MALTA

THE BLUE GUIDES

MALTA

STUART ROSSITER
M.A.

With 10 Maps and Plans

1968

LONDON: ERNEST BENN LIMITED
CHICAGO: RAND McNALLY & COMPANY

FIRST EDITION 1968

Published by Ernest Benn Limited
Bouverie House · Fleet Street · London · EC4

Rand McNally & Company
Chicago · Illinois 60680 · USA

© Ernest Benn Limited 1968

Printed in Great Britain

510–01551–4

PREFACE

MALTA, for more than a century and a half a British colony and fortified outpost of empire, has attracted the attention of tourists only since it became independent. This is all the more strange since for servicemen it was a popular station, the Maltese have always been well-disposed towards British visitors, and the island group affords equal opportunities, concentrated in a small area, for water-sports or sight-seeing. But military installations occupied much of the coast, and while the economy did not need civilian visitors hotel accommodation had remained inadequate. The 'run down' of the naval base changed the economic pattern of Maltese life at a moment when holidaymakers were ranging the Mediterranean for somewhere new to visit.

The BLUE GUIDE TO MALTA, a new volume in the series, is more than usually a pleasure for its editor to place before the public. For the idea, the necessary travel, and the compilation have been his own work to a degree unusual in the editing of guide books. The island, it is true, is well served by books both descriptive and scholarly, and a number of works, mostly locally produced, already minister to the visitor's needs. Nevertheless it is probably true to say that the multiform attractions of the island are here placed in the succinct form of a formal guide for the first time in English since the necessarily summary account of Murray's Handbook to the Mediterranean.

The earliest islanders quickly developed a skill in fashioning the limestone of which Malta is largely composed. The prehistoric temples are unique of their period alike for their topographical concentration, their complexity, and their state of preservation. Largely unaltered stand the splendid fortifications of the Knights of St John, built at a period when Italian military engineering had absorbed the scientific principles and the aesthetic feeling of the Renaissance. If these were generally designed by professionals from the mainland, their construction and the plans of the domestic buildings of the Order were usually entrusted to Maltese architects. Though their work derived broadly from the styles of Spain, France, and Sicily, it shows also marked local characteristics: a long tradition had already absorbed Siculo-Norman and Saracenic influences. Local craftsmanship survived the colonial period, the military buildings of which, erected mostly in high Victorian times, have a grace and strength more reminiscent of the 18C. With their deep arcading and often spectacular siting, they make a dis-tinguished and harmonious contribution to the landscape. Thus, with its long history paramount at every step, Malta has a fascination very much its own.

In an area roughly equivalent to that of the Isle of Wight are all the features of a full sovereign state. There are no great distances to travel and every corner of the islands is accessible. Paradoxically, however, the concentration of population, the complexity of the road system, and the ubiquitous stone terrace walls make Malta very confusing, while many unfamiliar constructions rouse the curiosity. The topography has therefore been described in rather greater detail than is usual in the Blue Guides, an attempt being made to satisfy the passing curiosity of the traveller as to the identity and historical interest of prominent and unfamiliar buildings even where these may be of limited artistic merit or banal present use. The reader should not assume that every building mentioned is worthy of a diversion in its own right, and may justly be satisfied to ignore what is not emphasized by bold type.

Though the prehistoric monuments of Malta have been objects of wonder for more than a century, they have until recently been widely misunderstood. Many of the conclusions of earlier archaeologists have been reversed in the last ten years. Even the latest and most reliable general books can be misleading. For this reason *Professor John D. Evans* of the Institute of Archaeology in the University of London was asked expressly for this book to write the essay that here appears under his name.

The maps and plans are wholly the work of *Mr John Flower*. The information there presented, while based immediately on editorial observation, owes much to the excellent maps of the Directorate of Overseas Surveys and to Baron Inguanez' pioneer Street Guide, to both of which acknowledgement is here made. The Editor is indebted to the Governor-General, *H. E. Sir Maurice Dorman*, and Lady Dorman for their kind hospitality and advice; to the staffs of the Malta Government Tourist Board and the National Museum at Valletta for information; and to the librarian of the Ministry of Defence (War Office) and the staff of the Public Record Office for assistance with historical detail of the 19C. Many useful references were made available by courtesy of the librarian of the Royal Commonwealth Society.

No one is better aware than the Editor of the difficulty of avoiding errors, and suggestions for the correction or improvement of the Guide will be most gratefully welcomed.

CONTENTS

MALTA

GOZO

MAPS AND PLANS

MAPS

PLANS

MALTA IN ANTIQUITY

by Professor J. D. EVANS

The beginnings of human occupation in the Maltese islands belong to the later part of the 5M B.C. Not until this relatively late date did a few boatloads of people, carrying with them their simple possessions, together with some seed corn and domestic animals, venture to cross the sixty odd miles of sea which separate the group from Sicily in order to take possession of this small, but still virgin, territory. The islands are visible in clear weather from Cape Passero at the s.e. tip of Sicily (which had been inhabited since the later part of the Palaeolithic period), and the crossing itself would not have presented any special difficulties in good weather conditions. Thus, in an unspectacular way, Maltese history began, a history which has been unexpectedly rich and varied; for, small as they are, and virtually destitute of natural resources, the Maltese islands can boast of a past more fascinating in itself, and often much more significant in a wider historical context, than that of many larger and richer countries. At several periods, indeed, they have played a role of vital importance to the fates of empires and even of continents! Before all this came about, however, the early inhabitants of the islands created some very remarkable cultures of their own, which, though of strictly local significance, are still of the greatest interest.

The prehistory of Malta can be divided into three main sections, each covering a little more than a thousand years, as follows:

Neolithic: Before 4000 B.C. to about 3000 B.C.

Copper Age: About 3000 B.C. to between 2000 and 1800 B.C.

Bronze Age: Between 2000 and 1800 B.C. to about 800 B.C.

Until recently a division of the prehistoric period into two parts only was usual, but the new discoveries of the last few years have made it desirable to separate off the later phases of the first of these divisions and to make a threefold classification, as set out above. It is a pity that the new terminology involves changing the name of the period during which the megalithic temples, by far the most famous of the prehistoric antiquities of Malta and Gozo, were erected. Though long known as the Maltese Neolithic, it has now been re-named the Copper Age. This slightly confusing change is not simply due to the perversity of archaeologists, but is dictated by the advance of knowledge, and the desirability of bringing the terminology of Maltese prehistory into line with that used to designate similar periods in neighbouring lands, especially Sicily.

Within each of the three periods of Maltese prehistory a number of finer subdivisions can be recognized. These phases, which vary considerably in length, are characterized chiefly by changing pottery styles, but also to some extent by changes in other aspects of the material equipment. The individual phases are each named after an archaeological site where material of that type was first found, or where it is particularly well represented. The dating of the periods and phases is now based chiefly on a series of radiocarbon dates which have been

9

obtained from samples collected from various sites in Malta, but chiefly from the recently excavated *Skorba* site. These give a rough absolute time-scale for Maltese prehistory as a whole, though they leave plenty of scope for argument about the dates for the beginning and end of individual phases, and even, to a lesser extent, of the three main periods. Apart from this, some links with datable archaeological material in other areas are also helpful from time to time, especially in the dating of the Bronze Age phases.

NEOLITHIC

Three phases are now recognized within this period. These are known as the *Għar Dalam*, *Grey Skorba* and *Red Skorba* phases. Until the recent excavations carried out by Dr D. H. Trump at the Skorba site only the first of these was known. This, the *Għar Dalam* phase, still represents what seems, so far as we know, to be the earliest occupation of the islands. The characteristic pottery is very distinctive, being brown or greyish in colour and often decorated with elaborate patterns which were impressed or incised in the wet surface of the clay before the pot was fired. Both the shapes and decoration of this *Impressed Ware*, as it is called, show a remarkably close resemblance to those made and used by the earliest Neolithic inhabitants of Sicily. The similarity is so great that it is clear that the earliest inhabitants of the Maltese islands must have sailed across from Sicily. The pottery of the two succeeding Skorba phases seems to develop quite naturally out of this tradition, without any sign of a break in the continuity. Nevertheless, there were considerable changes which came about in the course of time, notably the loss of the rich and elaborate impressed decoration. In fact, very little decoration occurs on the pottery of either of the Skorba phases, and when it does it is very simple. The shapes tend to be more angular, and a kind of ladle or dipper with a broad handle whose top is shaped like an M is very characteristic of both phases. The *Grey Skorba* phase is so named because the pottery is normally grey in colour, while during the *Red Skorba* phase a very striking red monochrome surface was developed.

The type site of the Għar Dalam phase is a natural cave, where there was found, in addition to the archaeological material, which was confined to the upper levels, a great mass of animal bones, including those of animals long extinct in the Maltese islands, such as elephant and hippopotamus, as well as red deer. These had been washed into the cave long before man appeared on the islands. Some human teeth also found here, which exhibit an abnormality which is fairly characteristic of those of Neanderthal man, seemed to suggest the presence of a group of Palaeolithic hunters until it was realized that the later prehistoric population of Malta had teeth which also exhibited this peculiarity fairly frequently.

It is uncertain whether the people who left their impressed pottery and flint implements at Għar Dalam used the cave to live in or simply for burying their dead, or perhaps for both purposes. The cave was also used by later people who seem to have disturbed the deposits left by the earliest people, so making it difficult to judge. Other caves occupied during the Għar Dalam phase are also known, but sherds of this pottery have also turned up from time to time on the sites of some of the megalithic temples. Probably these came from settlements in the open on sites later occupied by religious monuments, but it was not until the excavation of the Skorba site that the first remains of a village of this phase were brought to light. Part of an oval hut dating to the

Għar Dalam phase was found here, the foundations being of rough stones, the superstructure probably of wattle and daub or mud brick. A portion of a more massive wall, which ran in a straight line for a length of sixteen feet was also dated to this phase, though its purpose was not at all clear. The Skorba village continued to be inhabited through the following two phases, to which the site has given its name, but the chief architectural feature which has been uncovered belongs to the Red Skorba phase. This consists of two separate oval rooms, measuring about 26 ft by just over 17 ft, and constructed in very much the same way as the hut just described. However, these buildings do not seem to have been ordinary dwellings; the contents included a number of remarkable stylized figurines of clay representing female human figures, some goat skulls with horns attached, and some cow toe bones which had been rubbed down at one end to enable them to be set upright. This curious material suggests that they were probably shrines of some kind rather than ordinary domestic huts.

With regard to the way the Neolithic people disposed of their dead we are not well informed. As already noted, some of the human bones found in Għar Dalam may represent the remains of burials of this period, but it is impossible to be certain. A few fragments of human bone were found in the Skorba village, but they were not in any sense burials, and no other evidence is available.

The Neolithic people of Malta were farmers who had a long tradition of food-production behind them already when they arrived. Two pottery heads of what are probably sheep were found at Għar Dalam. They are of the characteristic grey fabric and may be parts of elaborate handles. Bones of sheep or goat, cow, pig and dog were found in the Għar Dalam levels at Skorba, and carbonized grains of barley, wheat and lentils were also found in them. A quern (or simple millstone) for grinding the grain was also found. Farming probably supplied the greater part of the food these early people ate, but they may well have varied their diet by collecting shell-fish (pierced shells were used as ornaments). The finding at Skorba of slingstones also suggests that they did a little hunting of whatever wild animals and birds were available.

From the first occupation of the Maltese islands by man it was necessary to import certain essential materials which were not to be found there. At this time stone was the only material known which provided effective cutting tools. Though local chert was available from which rough implements could be made, it was found worth while to import supplies of good flint from Sicily. Another material, obsidian, which is a natural glass found in volcanic deposits, makes superlatively sharp knives. It is of relatively rare occurrence, and was much prized and widely traded by Neolithic people. The Neolithic inhabitants of Malta and Gozo were obtaining supplies of this material from two different sources, the Lipari (or Aeolian) Islands, to the North of Sicily, and the island of Pantellaria to the w. The two types of obsidian have a distinctive appearance, but the provenance has also been confirmed by spectrographic analysis. The Lipari Islands were the more important source of the material, and as the period went on they, with their highly organized commerce, became the main suppliers of the Maltese islands. Lava was also imported into the islands, presumably from the area of Etna in Sicily, probably for making such things as querns. A small axe-shaped pendant of a green igneous stone found at Skorba must also have been imported.

Though the development of the pottery from the Għar Dalam to the Red Skorba phase seems to be a local one, it is noticeable that the red monochrome finish of the Red Skorba pottery is well matched in the Diana pottery of the Final Neolithic in the Lipari Islands and Sicily, and very similar lugs with expanded ends are found on both types. It seems likely that such convergence resulted from the close trading links between these areas. The Red Skorba phase is dated by radiocarbon in Malta to the later 4M B.C., and a similar date for the Diana type of pottery is well supported by a good deal of evidence.

COPPER AGE

The beginning of this period is marked by what appears to be a sharp break in the continuity of the cultural tradition in Malta. A new kind of pottery, the Żebbuġ ware, came into use, which is strikingly different from any of the Neolithic styles. For the first time, too, there is evidence that the dead were being buried collectively in artificially constructed tombs. It almost seems as though a new people had arrived to replace the earlier inhabitants, so complete is the change. Of course, archaeological evidence can sometimes be misleading in these matters, since fashions and customs can change without a change of population; but at all events the culture of the inhabitants of the Maltese islands took a completely new direction at this point, a direction which it continued to follow steadily for the next thousand years, and which eventually culminated in the construction and adornment of the great megalithic temples which are so famous throughout the world.

Five distinct phases can be recognized during the period, each characterized by distinct pottery style, though as in the Neolithic period an overall continuity of development can be discerned throughout. The stages are known as the *Żebbuġ, Mġarr, Ġgantija, Saflieni* and *Tarxien* phases.

The **Pottery** of the first of these is of two kinds, a dark mottled fabric, and a much lighter yellowish kind. Both kinds are decorated with lines deeply cut or incised into the surface of the clay, which were filled with a white or red paste to make them stand out. The most striking vases are jars with pear-shaped bodies and bell-like necks, which are sometimes decorated in a way which seems to show that they suggested human figures to their makers. This pottery is most closely similar to wares in use in Sicily at the beginning of the Copper Age there, and it may be that Sicilian influence was involved in its development.

The pottery of the *Mġarr* phase in Malta took the Żebbuġ type of decoration a stage further, substituting broad cut-out bands for the deep, narrow lines of the Żebbuġ style. The shapes, however, are simpler than in the earlier period.

In the following *Ġgantija* phase there was a further, and rather unexpected, development in the pottery decoration. The patterns were now made by scratching lines on the surface of the pot after it had been fired. Parts of these designs were hatched in the same technique, and finally an incrustation of red ochre was applied to the scratched lines and the hatched areas. The effect produced was that of a coloured pattern, the scratched lines being invisible on the finished product. The patterns are generally curvilinear, a favourite *motif* being two converging lines with a little circle at the point where they meet; it looks rather like a schematic representation of a comet with its tail of fire, though it is probably completely abstract. One kind of near-globular vase has the upper part entirely covered with a chequer-board pattern of squares, alternately left plain and filled with some kind of hatching or other decoration, while the lower part has the more common 'comet' type of decoration. The shapes of the pots are mostly rounded and rather baggy in this phase. As will be seen later, the Ġgantija phase was an important one and probably lasted a long time.

The *Saflieni* phase, on the other hand, seems to have been a short one. It has only been certainly identified as a separate chronological phase in the last few years, and it is still not very well known. The pottery is mostly in the Ġgantija tradition, though some new shapes, and even some new types of decoration appear. The scratched decoration continues, with both free curvilinear and chequer-board patterns, and is covered with red ochre as before. Some vases, however, have a surface which has been roughened by jabbing the wet clay all over with a bone point. The most striking new shapes are a flat based dish and a more or less biconical vessel known as the 'Saflieni' bowl. This is made in a wide variety of sizes. There are some extremely large, as well as some very miniaturized, examples. They are often elaborately decorated.

The final phase of the Copper Age is known as the *Tarxien* phase, and is named after the most elaborate of the temple-complexes, which belongs largely to this phase. The characteristic pottery is much more varied than that of any of the earlier ones. The standard decoration is still by scratched lines covered with red incrustation, but the patterns are different and much more elegant. They are usually based on a graceful volute *motif* and frequently recall the ornamental patterns popular in Middle Minoan Crete. Besides this, however, a whole range of new, and often elaborate techniques is used in the decoration of some of the pottery. These range from the use of applied studs or raised lumps set in a background of white paste inlay, to a kind of applied scale decoration which was used on large storage vessels. The forms of the pots in this phase tend to be angular, and frequently give the impression of being imitated from metal vessels, of which, however, no trace has yet been found in Malta. The Tarxien phase may have lasted a fairly long time, probably coming to a close fairly early in the 2M B.C. It represents the highest point of the Copper Age civilization of the Maltese islands.

Almost all our evidence concerning the Maltese people of the Copper Age comes from their **Tombs and Temples.** Until the excavation of the Skorba site nothing at all was known about their settlements, and this still remains the only village site of this period which has been located. Remains of huts of the Zebbuġ, Mġarr and Ġgantija phases were found at Skorba, which were all much the same in construction as the Neolithic ones. In shape they differed slightly, tending more towards the sub-rectangular. The floors were of beaten earth or *torba* (a plaster made of crushed limestone); the walls had stone footings, surmounted by mud brick and wattle and daub superstructures. Quernstones, and other remains suggestive of domestic activities, were found in them. In contrast to this scanty data about the everyday life of the people stands the great mass of evidence about their religious and funerary customs, though it is a pity that so much of this comes from important sites, including several of the most important temples, which were excavated (or rather cleared), before archaeology had developed as a science. Much evidence was destroyed in this early work, and many objects which were preserved are virtually without context.

The custom of burying the dead in collective tombs certainly goes back to the beginning of this period. It is illustrated by a group of five tombs which were accidentally discovered near the village of Zebbuġ. The Zebbuġ phase was named after this group of tombs. When found, they were shallow oval pits in the rock which contained numbers of broken and disarticulated human and animal bones, together with sherds of pottery, flint tools and bone and shell ornaments. In one there was also a roughly carved human head which had perhaps formed part of a statue or a gravestone. It is possible that these tombs had once been real chamber tombs, but had been partially destroyed later by minor quarrying operations of the kind that have always gone on in Malta. Some complete jars of the Żebbuġ style which survive in the National Museum and in private collections are most likely to have survived in tombs of this kind, though we know nothing for certain about where they came from. Such small chamber tombs, entered from a small circular pit, are known for certain to have been in use during the following, Mġarr, phase. Potsherds of this type were found in some of the tombs of a well-known group on the Xemxija Heights, above the N.W. side of St Paul's Bay, though most of the pottery found there dated from the Ġgantija and Tarxien phases.

It is clear that collective tombs of this simple kind were in use in Malta and Gozo throughout the Copper Age. In at least one instance, however, a much more elaborate kind of rock-cut burial place was constructed (or perhaps one might better say it evolved) over a long period of time. This is the famous Hal Saflieni Hypogeum, which consists of a remarkable agglomeration of halls and chambers cut out of the soft globigerina limestone. It seems to have contained the remains of not less than 6000 people, together with the grave-goods buried with them and probably some other material. Some of the smaller chambers which form a part of this strange monument are very much like single rock tombs of the type found at Xemxija, though generally larger and more carefully finished. The larger chambers and the great halls have a quite different character; they are richly adorned with painting and carving, the latter intended to reproduce underground the characteristics of the architecture of the megalithic temples. They are ceremonial, if not public, places. The germ of the development which produced Hal Saflieni is, however, to be seen at Xemxija, where two of the tombs are set side by side, and intercommunicate, though each has also its separate entrance. Pottery of all the Copper Age styles was found at Hal Saflieni, and this indicates how long its construction must have taken, since the carved halls imitate features of the temples erected in the later Ġgantija and Tarxien phases, while some of the painted ceilings resemble the decoration which first appears on pottery in the Tarxien phase.

Collective burial in rock-cut tombs is a fairly common kind of funerary custom around the shores of the Mediterranean, but the great megalithic temples of Malta and Gozo are unique. True, megalithic monuments are found in many other parts of the West Mediterranean and elsewhere in Western Europe, but they are normally communal graves, like the rock-tombs, not temples. So far as we know, none of the Maltese megalithic monuments were ever used for burial, though they were the locus of an elaborate cult which was evidently very closely linked with the ancestors buried in the rock-tombs and the Hal Saflieni Hypogeum. It is even likely that the peculiar form of the temples, based on clusters of semicircular or horseshoe-shaped rooms, derives ultimately from the form of some of the burial chambers. The largest of the tombs at Xemxija, Tomb 5, has a curious lobed plan, which seems to have been dictated by the necessity of leaving portions of rock standing in order to support the roof, which might otherwise have collapsed. These divided the rear part of the room into a chamber of curved spaces. This plan is very similar to that of the most primitive of the surviving shrines, the smaller of the two buildings which make up the temple at Ta Haġrat (Mġarr), though there was no functional necessity for such a plan.

Though the temples were not used for burial, the Hypogeum was certainly used for some sort of religious purposes and this provides some further evidence for the complex links between the tombs and the temples. There may even have been a megalithic building in front of the original entrance to the Hypogeum. However, none of the surviving temples can be shown to date from the earlier phases of the Copper Age. They seem all to have been built, or at least to have reached their present form, in the Ġgantija and later phases. Like the Hypogeum, however, the Maltese temples were complex structures which were subject to periodic alteration, rebuilding and extension over a long period of time. This piecemeal construction often makes it difficult for us to trace their full history. A good analogy is the complicated architectural history of many European churches and cathedrals.

Most of the temple-complexes consist of one or more separate 'units', each having its own entrance which leads into a group of three or more rooms arranged around one or more square or rectangular courts, though a few are more irregular structures. In form and technique of building the most primitive of the surviving monuments are the two known as Ta Ħaġrat in the village of Mġarr. As already mentioned, the smaller of these, built of rough stones, has a plan which is reminiscent of a large rock-cut tomb. The bigger building marks a considerable advance on this. In plan it is trefoil-shaped, having three separate chambers all opening off a rectangular paved court. Two of these are roughly circular, while the third is really a kind of irregular space off which opens the entrance to the smaller building. The entrance to the larger building, which serves also as the entrance to the whole monument, is set in the centre of a concave façade, a feature which is found in megalithic architecture in various parts of western Europe. The whole building is surrounded by an outer wall, between which and the chambers inside is a packing of earth and stones. This building is in essence the model for all the later temples.

A very similar trefoil temple can be seen in the Kordin III complex, though it seems a little more developed in that, instead of the circular chambers, there are semicircular rooms which are fenced off from the central court by stone partitions. This building shares a common façade with one which looks rather like a throw-back to a much earlier type, since it has a rather indeterminate lobed plan. The next development is illustrated by the massive monument appropriately known as the Ġgantija, situated near the village of Xagħra, in Gozo. Here two 'units' stand side by side, sharing a common façade. Each of them has five rooms instead of three, and they are arranged round two courts joined by a short corridor. There are, however, some significant differences between these two 'units', and the southernmost seems to be the earlier. Its three rear rooms, arranged in the usual trefoil pattern, are much larger than the two front ones, which is the opposite of what is normally found in units with five or more rooms. It almost seems as though the front rooms were added here as an afterthought.

The northern 'unit', on the other hand, has a more orthodox plan. The two rooms which lie on either side of the first court are larger than those at the back, while the rear room, which faces the entrance, has begun to shrink in size; it is already quite small and is filled up by a kind of niche built of slabs. Excavations have shown that these two 'units' were both erected during the Ġgantija phase, though the niche in the northern one seems to have been added during the Tarxien phase.

Apart from one example in the Tarxien complex, the 'units' which go to make up the later temple-complexes mostly resemble the northern building of the Ġgantija pair very closely in plan, save that the old rear room was even further reduced in size, so that it is only just big enough to accommodate a small niche. The exception is the central building of the main group at Tarxien, which has three pairs of lateral semicircular chambers, instead of the usual two. This may be partly, if not entirely, explained by the necessity of filling the space between the other two buildings, and the first pair of rooms are really more like an oval court. A wholly exceptional complex is the main group of buildings at Ḥaġar Qim, where we seem to have the remains of one orthodox 'unit', which has, however, been altered so as to have an entrance at the back as well as the front, while on the w. side of it there has grown up a very irregular complex of oval rooms. This complex seems to have been entirely constructed during the Ġgantija phase, but it does not fit into any scheme of development.

The megalithic buildings show evidence of the progressive development in the skill and ambition of their builders. The early ones, like those at Ta Ḥaġrat, are constructed of rough boulders and slabs of coralline limestone. This technique of construction is also seen, on a much larger scale, in both the Ġgantija buildings, though here dressed blocks and slabs of the softer globigerina limestone were also used in certain places, while the outer casing was made of huge slabs of coralline limestone, surmounted by courses of blocks. The walls of the rooms were originally finished by covering them with a mass of clay, capped with a coat of lime plaster which was painted red. Traces of this covering have been found adhering to the walls at some points. In later buildings upright slabs surmounted by coursed blocks were used for the construction of both inner and outer walls. The harder coralline limestone was still preferred for the outer casing, but for the interior the softer globigerina limestone, which could be cut and dressed exactly to shape was used. There is no evidence that plaster was used to surface the walls of these later temples, and indeed none would be needed, so fine is the finish and the fitting of the slabs.

Even in the most primitive of the surviving monuments the walls of the chambers, in so far as they survive, show signs of curving inwards to form some sort of vault. In the later buildings the slabs which form the lower part of the walls often lean slightly inwards, while the courses of dressed blocks which surmounted them were corbelled. Each course slightly overlapped the one below, thus gradually reducing the total space to be roofed. Some of the smaller monuments might have been roofed entirely with stone in this way, or by finishing off with a stone slab or slabs at a certain height. But the Maltese building stone will not span a space of more than about 7 ft without intermediate support. There is no evidence of the existence of such supports in the larger temples, and it seems quite impossible that their rooms can have been roofed in this manner. Moreover, traces of the huge slabs employed would surely have been found. So either they were open to the sky, in which case the courses of carefully corbelled blocks seem a curiously elaborate waste of labour, or else they were roofed with some perishable material, such as wood. This solution seems to be supported by the marks of a fierce conflagration which can be seen on the walls of some of the buildings at Tarxien, and also by the remarkably good state of preservation of some of the delicate carvings found there and in other temples, which seems surprising if they were exposed to the elements.

The pattern of occurrence of these carved blocks is interesting in itself. None are found in the remains of the Ta Ḥaġrat or Kordin III monuments, or in other buildings which seem to belong to early stages on the development of the temples. There are a few in the South building at the Ġgantija and at Ḥaġar Qim, but even these could well have been added after the original construction of the monuments. They are not an integral part of the construction, and some of them feature spiral patterns which seem appropriate only to the Tarxien phase. The earliest decoration employed was probably a sort of honeycomb pattern produced by pitting or drilling the surface. Some of the blocks originally decorated in this way were re-used later to carry spiral patterns, but occasionally some of the original pitting survives.

These amazing constructions were quite clearly temples, in the sense of being designed especially for the celebration of a cult. This seems to have become more and more elaborate as time went on, necessitating corresponding elaboration of the plan of the temples. As already suggested, the cult seems to have been closely connected with the dead, but it also involved at least one divine being, represented as a preternaturally fat, but sexless, figure in the numerous statuettes and figurines which have been found. These figures are generally naked, but some are clothed from the waist down in a full, fringed skirt which reaches to the calves.

Animal sacrifices obviously played a large part in the worship which took place in the temples. The five-roomed 'units' of the later ones are always equipped with a pair of altar-like constructions which flank the entrance to the corridor that leads from the front to the rear rooms. The right-hand altar of such a pair in the s.w. 'unit' of the Tarxien complex, which is elaborately decorated with spiral patterns in relief, proved to be hollow. The interior was found to be filled with the burnt bones of sacrificed animals, while behind a neat stone plug which covered an opening in the front of the altar lay a curved stone knife, obviously the sacrificial instrument, reposing just where it had been carefully replaced after the last sacrifice. Numerous small cupboards and niches of stone slabs which have been found in various parts of the temples were usually full of burnt animal bones when found. Sheep, goat, pig and cow were all sacrificed, and in the Tarxien temples there were lively carvings of all of them on slabs and blocks found in various parts of the temples. To judge by some rough drawings on potsherds and a small stone head, snakes also played some part, though perhaps only a minor one. Circular holes pierced through some of the paving and threshold slabs into the ground below may have had to do with drink offerings, and in this connection it is interesting to note that thousands of fragments of a special type of handled bowl have been found in all the temples. Could they have been the ones which were used for the libations and then ceremoniously broken?

Such an elaborate religion is likely to have been highly organized, and almost certainly it had its priestly caste, whether these were full time officials or not. Traces of the existence of such an order have been found at Tarxien. There a large part of the middle temple 'unit' is separated off by a slab set up on edge, blocking the corridor which leads to the second and third sets of rooms. This slab is carved with a double spiral design which may symbolize a pair of watchful eyes which were intended to ward off the profane. A staircase led to an elevated corridor which ran behind the walls of these rooms. Originally there was doubtless a special entrance to them from this, but that part of the building has suffered much destruction and the evidence has been obliterated.

In two of the temple complexes, Tarxien and Mnajdra, small rooms have been discovered between the inner and outer walls. These were entered from the exterior and communicated with the temple only by means of a small rectangular opening in one of the wall slabs. They have been, no doubt correctly, interpreted as arrangements for the delivery of an oracle or some other kind of priestly mystification. At Tarxien remains of some clay figures were found which represented

B

full-bodied men clothed from the waist down in elaborate pleated skirts which reached to their feet. Two of these have well-modelled heads with strongly marked features which may be portraits. It has been suggested that they represent priests of the cult. In the Hal Saflieni Hypogeum, which, as already noted, was used for certain religious and ceremonial purposes as well as for burial, two small models representing women, also clothed in decorated skirts, and reclining on well-modelled beds, were found. These odd finds may show us something which actually happened there, since we know that in Classical times sleeping in caves or other sacred places in order to obtain prophetic dreams—incubation, as it is called—was a familiar occurrence, in which priestesses were often involved.

In some of the temples at least there may have been a healing cult, as well as the main one connected with the dead and the divine figure. A number of figurines have been found apparently showing people suffering from a variety of ailments, as well as models of individual human limbs. It is all very reminiscent of the *ex votos* found in Classical sanctuaries, or still to be seen in Christian churches, especially in Mediterranean lands.

Though they give us a vivid picture of a society dominated by a religion to whose service it could and did divert an enormous amount of time and labour, the temples and tombs tell us very little about the more mundane side of life in Malta at this period. The sheer organization necessary for the planning and erection of the temples, and the evidence for the existence of priests and perhaps priestesses, suggest some degree of social complexity. The stone carvers, modellers and sculptors employed in the construction and adornment of the temples may well have been specialist craftsmen living off the produce of the farming community, as would also the priests themselves. The models of buildings or parts of buildings which have been found in several of the temples, together with the curious fragment of what seems to be a plan of a building (not a temple, but one with rectangular rooms) which was found at Tarxien, might even suggest that there were specialist architects. Recent study of the human bones found in the Xemxija tombs takes us even further. These bones are those of lightly built people with little muscular development, such as might be expected to come from regular manual work. It does not seem possible, therefore, that these can be the people who actually built the temples, or even tilled the fields. Perhaps burial in the rock tombs or the Hypogeum was reserved for members of a specially privileged class, and in this case the temple worship may have been for their benefit too.

Despite the use of the term Copper Age for this period of Maltese prehistory there is no evidence at present of the use of metal tools of any kind in the Maltese islands at this time. It would still be rash to conclude that they did not know of such things. A taboo on the use of metal objects in the temples is quite feasible, and we still know too little about the settlements to be sure what went on there. For the moment, however, the justification of the term Copper Age as applied to this period is simply that of convenience.

The chief tools employed in the construction of the monuments of this period were antler picks or wedges, which were used in conjunction with heavy stone mallets. These were used for hewing the rock in the Hypogeum, and probably also for the quarrying and rough shaping of the slabs for the temples. For the finer dressing, and probably also for carving, flint or obsidian blades would have been employed. The heavy slabs for the temples were moved by means of heavy balls of limestone which acted like ball-bearings, and of which many have been found on the temple sites. Ropes, which of course have not survived, were no doubt employed in conjunction with these. The slabs were raised into position with the aid of levers, probably wooden, for which sockets can still be seen on some of them.

Pendants of hard green stone in the shape of miniature axes are common finds, though real stone axes seem to have been extremely rare. But so are the stone mallets, and once more perhaps the situation would be different if we knew more settlement sites. Scrapers of flint and chert may have been used as wood planes, though they were no doubt also employed for skin dressing. Apart from scrapers, the most common flint and obsidian tools are knives, of which some very fine examples are known. The only weapons were biconical limestone slingstones (if that is really what they are), which may have been used in hunting.

A flourishing weaving industry is attested by finds of clay spindle-whorls, as well as by the models of figures clothed in elaborate skirts. It is possible that fine textiles may have been exported to pay for some of the materials which the Maltese had to obtain abroad, such as flint and obsidian (the former from Sicily, as before, the latter now exclusively from Lipari), lava for querns and igneous stone for axes, axependants, etc. All these imported raw materials probably came from relatively near at hand, from Sicily, from other Italian islands or from the mainland itself. However, there is some evidence for wider contacts, particularly in the second half of the Maltese Copper Age. There are striking resemblances between Maltese pottery of the Tarxien phase and the contemporary Copper Age culture of Sardinia, the Ozieri culture, while both the Maltese and Sardinian cultures produced figurines which closely resemble types developed in the Cyclades and widely traded in the Aegean area during the later 3M B.C. But the material of both the Tarxien people of Malta and the Ozieri people of Sardinia also has some notable similarities to that of Middle Minoan Crete, which suggests that they may both have been in part contemporary with this period, which covered the first half of the 2M B.C.

BRONZE AGE

The great era of Maltese prehistory came to an end with the close of the Copper Age, and from one point of view everything else seems to be anticlimax. The Hypogeum and the great temples went out of use, and the highly developed art disappeared. The Bronze Age cultures have their own fascination, but they produced nothing comparable with the artistic and architectural achievement of the Copper Age. The Maltese Bronze Age can be divided into three main phases, but unlike those of the Neolithic and Copper Age they do not represent the continuous development of a single tradition, but rather a series of separate colonizations of the islands by people who came from elsewhere.

The first of these intrusive cultures is that of the *Tarxien Cemetery* people, so named after the large cremation cemetery which was the first site of this culture found. It was discovered by Sir T. Zammit in the course of his excavation of the Tarxien temples in 1915, and it is still by far the richest and most important one known. What happened to the flourishing Copper Age population is unknown, but it is clear that when the cemetery was formed at Tarxien the temples had gone out of use. If the tombs and temples were erected for the benefit of a privileged and powerful minority, then their abandonment need not mean a complete change of population, merely the replacement of the old oligarchs by new rulers. But whether numerous or not, the new people had completely different customs and equipment. Their cemetery consisted of a large number of cremations which were placed in large urns together with remains of clothing, ornaments, tools, weapons and pottery. A level platform had first been created by covering the floors of the old building with sand to a depth of about three feet, and it was on this that the material was found. Signs of burning over the whole area indicated that the cremation of the bodies (which was usually very imperfect) may have taken place on the spot, perhaps using old timbers from the roofing of the temples.

The objects found with the burials were numerous. Especially so were pots, of which over 200 complete examples were found. Many were decorated with incised, white-filled lines which formed rectilinear geometric patterns. Fragments of a loosely-woven fabric, probably originally dyed, were found, but these were not large enough to give any idea of the kind of garments worn. Beads and pendants of stone, ostrich-shell, faience, clay and even fish-vertebrae were present in large numbers.

A series of stylized clay figurines representing female figures seated on stools was found. Most of these are so schematized that it would be difficult to know what they were but for two more detailed and lifelike examples which are quite recognizably female human figures, though still very stylized. Both are wearing an elaborate headdress. Metal objects occur for the first time in Malta. Copper awls set in bone handles and probably also some copper axes were tools, but a series of triangular copper daggers which were found were quite possibly weapons. The bow was certainly in use as a weapon at this time, as shown by a few obsidian arrow-heads. These come from various sites, but probably all belong to the Tarxien Cemetery people, who seem to have been quite distinctly more warlike than previous inhabitants of Malta.

Though the characteristic pottery of the Tarxien Cemetery people has been found on a number of sites in Malta and Gozo (including the Skorba temples), most of the known material is still from the Tarxien site. The only monuments which they can be shown to have built themselves are some small and very rough structures, usually called 'dolmens', of which a number are known on both Malta and Gozo. They consist of a rough slab of coralline limestone between three and ten feet in length, which is supported a little above ground level by a series of slabs on edge or of pillars composed of several small blocks. Sometimes the capstone has a hole pierced vertically through it, and in one or two instances grooves are also to be seen on the upper surface. The rock below the capstone has sometimes been hollowed out to increase the height of the chamber. There is no trace in any instance of a mound which might have covered these structures, and most now stand on bare rock. One of them, situated at Ta Hammut, did however contain a little soil, which, when excavated, yielded some sherds of the typical pottery. A curious trapezoidal cairn at Wied Moqbol on the s. coast also produced some sherds of Tarxien Cemetery type. No human bones were found in either of these monuments but it is possible that they may have originally contained cremation burials.

The characteristic pottery of the Tarxien Cemetery people is similar in many ways to the pottery used by the contemporary Early Bronze Age people of the Lipari Islands. Significant resemblances have also been noted between the pottery of both these groups and that used by some of the people of W. Greece in the late 3 and earlier 2M B.C. It seems likely that both groups had their ultimate origin in Greece, though the Tarxien Cemetery people at least may well have spent some time in the heel of Italy before their arrival in Malta. The evidence for this is the existence in the area around Otranto of structures which closely resemble the Maltese 'dolmens', even to the perforated capstones and groovings. Unfortunately no pottery has been found associated with many of these S. Italian monuments, but material resembling that of the Tarxien Cemetery culture has now been found on a number of sites in the E. part of Sicily, so that they may have also touched there before finally coming to Malta.

The fate of the Tarxien Cemetery people is as problematic as their origin. All that can be said for certain is that in the later 2M B.C. we find the Maltese islands in the hands of people who were using a new kind of equipment, but it may be that once more this betokens a change in the ruling group rather than in the mass of the population. The new culture takes its name from *Borġ in-Nadur*, which is the site of a settlement of the period situated close to St George's Bay in the Marsaxlokk. It occupies a triangular area of land between two converging *wieds* (or dry torrent beds). On two sides these valleys seem to have been thought to offer sufficient protection, but on the third side are the remains of a huge defensive wall with a massive central redoubt. Though it has not been possible to investigate the area of the settlement on a large scale, some oval huts with stone foundations have been located in the part just behind the defensive wall. In the S. corner of the triangular space delimited by the wall are the remains of a Copper Age temple-complex. When this was excavated in the 1920s it became clear that the ruins had been used in the Borġ in-Nadur phase for domestic purposes. Probably, then, the settlement was a large one, occupying more or less the whole of the space available, Recent excavations just behind the defensive wall have shown that the site may also have been occupied as a settlement already in the Tarxien Cemetery phase. A number of other settlements of the Borġ in-Nadur phase are known in Malta and Gozo, invariably sited on hilltops or other high and easily defensible ground. Some of them also have remains of defensive walls, though none on such a scale as that of Borġ in-Nadur itself.

The typical Borġ in-Nadur pottery has a shiny red surface which, however, flakes off easily to reveal a buff-coloured fabric below. Decoration is by deeply cut lines which have a square section, as though cut by a small chisel. They form simple but highly individual patterns which were filled with white paste. On some pots the red slip was used to make rough patterns instead of being applied all over. Shapes are two-handled bowls or cups which are often set on a high conical foot, high-handled bowls, cups and jugs, footed lamps, and small vases with elaborate T-shaped or axe-shaped handles. A very peculiar vessel is a rectangular basin with internal divisions, a characteristic also found occasionally in the very different Tarxien Cemetery ware.

Identical pottery has been found in the rock-cut tombs of certain cemeteries in the Syracuse district of Sicily, where it is associated with the local grey pottery, but also with Mycenaean pottery of the 14C B.C. Though these vases may well be imports from Malta, it seems evident that the tradition of potting which produced the Borġ in-Nadur wares originally stems from Sicily, where a tradition of red-slipped wares began in the Copper Age, in which period also similar divided basins are found. A single sherd of Mycenaean pottery datable to the 13C B.C. was found at Borġ in-Nadur, and what is possibly a second one was found in the recent Italian excavations at Tas Silġ.

A great many of the bell-shaped pits which are to be found cut into the rock all over Malta and Gozo may well date from the Borġ in-

Nadur phase. Numbers of them occur near the settlements of this period and some have been found to contain the characteristic pottery. They were used doubtless for storing water and grain. Many others are probably later in date, since this kind of cistern or silo was in use in Malta at all later periods. The mysterious 'cart-tracks' (which in reality were probably ruts made by slide-cars, not wheeled vehicles) may also belong to this period. Some of them are to be found quite near the settlements of the Borġ in-Nadur people.

Apart from their agricultural activities the Borġ in-Nadur people carried on a busy weaving industry, as shown by the numerous spindle and loom weights of clay which have been found in their settlements. The curious clay anchor-shaped objects also found may well have used in connection with some process of this industry, too. Small fragments of bronze, and a mould for making a bronze ornament found at Borġ in-Nadur show that by now at any rate metal working was taking place on the islands. But finds of metal are still rare, which is not surprising, since it must still have been a costly imported material, not lightly to be discarded when it could be so easily re-used. No doubt old and broken metal objects were carefully collected and melted down by the smiths.

The Borġ in-Nadur culture survived for a long time in Malta. Recent work has made it possible to recognize three chronological subdivisions, each characterized by changes in the pottery. The final phase seems to have lasted down to about 800 B.C., or in other words to the end of the true prehistoric period. Thus the last of the three groups of intrusive Bronze Age people do not represent a separate chronological phase, but were contemporary with the late Borġ in-Nadur people. This group is known as the *Baħrija* culture, taking its name from a settlement site in the S.W. of Malta which seems in fact to be the only centre of this culture. Even at this site some of the pottery is clearly of Borġ in-Nadur type, and recent excavation work there has shown that it was originally a settlement of the Borġ in-Nadur people.

The typical Baħrija pottery has a black or grey surface. Some of it is nevertheless obviously derived from the Borġ in-Nadur tradition. The decoration is in the old 'chiselled' style, but includes the use of chip-carving (originally a technique used for decorating wooden vessels) and of patterns such as maeanders which were not known to the Borġ in-Nadur potters. Other vases, notably a series of angular bowls, are obviously foreign to Maltese tradition, though they have the same kind of decoration as the rest. There are also sherds of a new kind of painted ware.

The new decorative features and shapes point very clearly to the arrival of people coming from some part of South Italy. Presumably this was just a small group of immigrants who settled at the Baħrija site, where they succeeded in transforming the culture of the local inhabitants to some extent. Several objects found at Baħrija seem to confirm that the immigrants were of South Italian origin, such as fragments of rough pottery 'cheese-strainers', well known in South Italy, where pastoral activities had long been of paramount importance. A decorated clay weight, possibly a very large loom-weight, also has exact parallels in Calabria.

That the Baħrija people had contacts with the Borġ in-Nadur inhabitants of the other settlements is clearly shown by the occurrence of stray fragments of the typical black pottery at a number of them. Just why the immigrants should have chosen to settle at Baħrija is something of a mystery, since there is no convenient harbour nearby. Surprisingly enough, though, the inhabitants of the Baħrija settlement seem to have been richer than their neighbours in one way—they could afford to acquire more metal objects (at least to judge by the number of small fragments of metal which they lost or threw away). Finds of spindle-whorls, loom-weights and clay anchors were also far more numerous than at other sites, which might suggest that Baḥrija was a centre for the industrial production of textiles for export. Perhaps the immigrant group from Italy was in some way specially connected with this trade.

The preference of the later Bronze Age inhabitants of Malta for settlements on inaccessible hilltops or defended by massive walls would seem to imply an unsettled state of affairs which lasted for several centuries. This emphasis on defence could reflect the danger of pirate raids, so often an important factor in Mediterranean life, or it could reflect an internal political situation in which each group, with its fortified settlement, was independent of, and potentially hostile to, every other. There may be some truth in both these explanations, but we shall probably never be able to find a definitive solution. In contrast to the ubiquitous fortifications, there has been a complete absence of finds of weapons, but since these would have been of bronze, they were no doubt melted down when they ceased to be of use.

PHOENICIAN AND PUNIC PERIODS

Though the earliest material of Phoenician type which has been found in Malta dates from the 8C B.C., no written documents which bear on the islands' history are available until much later. For another few centuries they were still virtually in a prehistoric stage. The early Phoenician material comes from rock-cut tombs, which continued to be the norm for burial right through the Punic and into the Roman period. A great mass of material has been found in the large number of such tombs which have come to light. The earliest are circular in plan, with a circular pit entrance. Later first the pit, then the chamber itself come to be square or rectangular in form.

Just how and why the Phoenicians first came to the Maltese islands we do not know. Probably they found the harbours useful as refuges from storms and pirates on their trading voyages to the w. The name Malta itself may come from the Phoenician *malat*, a port or refuge, but we do not know for certain that the Phoenicians called it by this name. They certainly called Gozo *gol*, which means a broad-beamed merchant ship, and there is some evidence that their name for Malta may have been *'onan*, a large ship. Perhaps they thought of the islands as a fleet of ships of different sizes! It seems possible that the flourishing textile industry of late prehistoric times may also have had something to do with their interest, however. Centuries later, in Roman times, the manufacture of fine textiles was still one of the staples of the islands' prosperity.

Some of these early Phoencians did settle and were buried on the islands, but it is difficult to say just what their status was, or how far they were in control. They must have been in contact with the native inhabitants, but there is remarkably little evidence available bearing on this question. Many years ago a settlement site was investigated at Qallilija, near Mdina, which produced Late Bronze Age and Phoenician material, and stray objects of Phoenician type have been found on other Bronze Age sites, but this does not take us very far.

Another problem of this shadowy period is what relations the early Greek traders and colonists had with the Maltese islands at this time, if any. A certain number of Proto-Corinthian, Corinthian and Black

Figure vases have been found in Malta, but these do not necessarily imply anything more than occasional trading, presumably with the Greek colonies of Sicily. The idea that there was a Greek colonization of the islands during the 7 or 6C B.C. rests almost entirely on a mistaken dating of Greek inscriptions and Maltese coins which really belong to the time when the islands had come under Roman domination.

Whatever the uncertainties as to the history of the Maltese islands during the 8 and 7C B.C., it is certain that in the course of the 6C B.C. they passed into the hands of Carthage, originally a Phoenician colony, which was at that time building up a trading empire in the West Mediterranean. For the first time in their history but by no means the last, the islands became of strategic importance. The Carthaginians were in process of consolidating their power in Sicily and the Gulf of Syrte, so that possession of the small, centrally placed island group became of vital importance to them in connection with their efforts to withstand Greek advance in this area.

For more than three centuries after this the Maltese islands remained a part of the Punic Empire. It seems very likely that the Carthaginians actually sent colonists to settle the islands, though we have no certain knowledge about this. The archaeological evidence is of no help in assessing the size of such a colony, since all the equipment used in this period seems to have been of Punic type, with, in the later part of the period, a growing number of imported Greek objects. However, it is noticeable that the islands seem to have been allowed a greater degree of freedom than most Punic satellites. For instance, they seem to have been allowed to trade freely with foreigners, which was most unusual. The Greek imports, and conversely the early popularity of the Maltese dog in the Greek world, are good evidence for this. Towards the end of the Punic period the Maltese seem to have even been allowed to strike their own coins, if scholars are correct in dating the first issues before the Roman occupation.

As already mentioned, most of the archaeological evidence for the Punic period comes from the rock-tombs. The objects which accompany the burials are mostly dull and repetitious, with occasional exceptions, which are usually imported Greek or Egyptian objects. One tomb yielded a fine clay sarcophagus which is a quite early example of a well-known Punic type which is based on the Egyptian mummy-case. The lid of this example is moulded into the shape of a female figure.

It has long been known from documentary evidence and from inscriptions in the Phoenician language found in Malta and Gozo, that the Carthaginians established important temples to their gods in both islands. There was known to be one in Malta dedicated to Melkart (later identified with the Graeco-Roman Herakles or Hercules), and another to his consort Astarte (the Greek Hera, Roman Juno). In the last few years large scale excavations by the University of Rome at the hill of Tas Silġ, near Marsaxlokk, have revealed that this was the site of the latter. This Punic temple was found to have been constructed over the remains of a Copper Age sanctuary, among whose ruins was found one of the characteristic stone statues of a fat sexless deity. The Punic building was a well-built complex of halls and courts of rectangular plan, with a store for the bones of sacrificed animals and for a large number of potsherds bearing dedications to two goddesses, Astarte and Tanit. These provided positive identification of the building. There was a ramp leading from the temple on its hill down to the port on the coast not far away.

The temple of Melkart was probably in the near neighbourhood of the Astarte-Tanit temple, since as long ago as the 17th century a stone *cippus* (small column) with a votive inscription to Melkart was found in the vicinity. This object has a special importance because the in-scription recording the dedication by two brothers, Abdosir and Osirxamar, was cut into the base of the column in both Phoenician and Greek, and this bilingual helped considerably in the first de-cypherment of the Phoenician language. It is now in the Louvre. Another Phoenician inscription refers to the restoration of various temples in Gozo by the people of that island.

About the settlements of this period we know very little, probably because their remains now lie under modern towns and villages. We know that in Malta there were important ones at Mdina, Marsaxlokk and Birgu, but there were obviously others also. In the village of Żurrieq, for example, there is a very remarkable survival which could be a relic of pre-Roman architecture. The main part is a tower about 24 ft high made of massive rectangular blocks carefully dressed and well fitted together. This structure is crowned by a deep overhanging cornice which gives the building something of an Egyptian effect. This tower is now incorporated in one of the houses of the village, and some remains of other walls of similar character show that it was originally part of a set of rooms grouped round a rectangular courtyard.

The development of Roman power and the growing rivalry between Rome and Carthage brought on a period of unrest and suffering for the inhabitants of the Maltese islands during the 3C B.C. In the year 257 B.C., during the First Punic War, Malta was invaded by a Roman army under the Consul C. Attilius Regulus, and was thoroughly de-vastated and plundered. The Romans may have intended to occupy the islands permanently at this time, but if so their defeat in Africa two years later put an end to the plan and the Carthaginians returned and continued to hold them until 218 B.C. In that year, at the beginning of the Second Punic War, a Roman force under Sempronius finally took possession of the islands, apparently without a struggle, and probably with the connivance of the inhabitants, who handed them over, along with the Punic garrison, to the Roman consul.

ROMAN PERIOD

The Romans incorporated the Maltese islands into the province of Sicily. The archaeological evidence shows clearly that while the Punic culture and speech of the local people was at first little affected by the new political situation, a Greek element appeared which was of con-siderable importance, as shown by the striking number of inscriptions in Greek. It was even thought desirable to put a Greek translation of the dedication on the *cippus* of Abdosir and Osirxamar, already mentioned above, which probably dates from the 2C B.C. This situation is easily understandable, since the influence of the important Greek cities of Sicily was bound to be strong in the new situation. However, the great majority of the population undoubtedly continued to speak their native Punic dialect, just as Maltese is spoken at the present day. Whether this Semitic speech survived up to the time of the Arab in-vasion in the 9C A.D. is not known, but it seems perfectly possible. Such a survival would certainly make the rapid adoption of another Semitic language at that time more easily understandable.

The burials in the rock-tombs give us the same picture of the per-sistence of Punic tradition, which was only gradually modified by the influence of Graeco-Roman civilization. Cremation as well as inhuma-tion is found in the tombs of the earlier Roman period, and objects of Greek or Roman manufacture or design occur in them mixed with objects, especially pottery, of Punic type. The tombs were often used and re-used over a long period, the earlier burials being simply pushed to the back. Clay oil lamps, which were always left lighted when the tomb was sealed, illustrate this continuity very vividly, since types of very different dates are sometimes found in the same tomb.

As time went on more elaborate types of rock-tomb were sometimes made, which were in the nature of small cemeteries incorporating a number of separate burial places for one or two bodies. These may sometimes have been owned by families, but others were those of guilds. One at Rabat seems to have been the property of a guild of weavers, to judge by the carvings of weaving equipment in the central hall; others of masons, tinsmiths, etc. Many of the simpler of these hypogea consist only of two short corridors, or a single hall, the individual graves opening about half way up the walls. Some, however, are more elaborate, consisting of an irregular collection of rooms, often having a small hall with a semicircular apse as the nodal point. These are often equipped with stone benches and a stone table, perhaps intended for the sharing of a funeral meal. The more elaborate of these rock cemeteries seem to date from the 4 and 5C A.D., though some may be older. The largest and most elaborate are the St Paul's Catacombs at Rabat. These seem to be definitely of Christian origin, and a few others can be ascribed to Christian communities with a similar confidence. Most produced no evidence bearing on the religion of their users, but many of these also may have been Christian. A few were probably owned by Jewish communities. None of the Maltese catacombs compare in size with those of Rome; in detail, they are most closely similar to those of Sicily.

The temples founded during the Punic period long kept their importance, and indeed seem to have attained, during the earlier part of the Roman period, an even greater international fame than they had earlier. So much has long been known from the references by Cicero in his prosecution of the infamous Verres, who was propraetor of Sicily (including the Maltese islands) from 73–71 B.C., for abusing his position and organizing the systematic pillaging of his province. Cicero refers specifically to his depradations on the treasures of the famous temples of Proserpine, Apollo and Juno in Malta. This last would now seem to have been identified in the temple uncovered by the Italian excavators at Tas Silġ. Here the Punic temple of Astarte-Tanit was extended on a lavish scale in Roman times. The new complex included a monumental portico and a fine mosaic pavement. Fragments of votive plaques of this period bear dedications to Hera (the Greek form of Juno, and also identified with Astarte). The temple of Juno seems to have recovered from Verres' spoliations, however, and continued to flourish for some time. During the 2C A.D. it seems finally to have been abandoned, and somewhere between the 4 and 6Cs A.D. a Christian monastery was erected on the site. The baptistery of this was situated right over the centre of the old temple, but other parts, including the church, have not yet been located.

The chief town in Malta during Roman times was on the site of the present day Mdina and part of Rabat. This had previously been the old Punic capital, so no change was involved. The large number of tombs and catacombs found in the area of Rabat confirm its importance. They lie just outside the area covered by the Roman town (which was somewhat larger than the present Mdina), in accordance with the Roman regulation forbidding burial of the dead in a town. Some vestiges of an important house of the Roman period have been uncovered, and a Museum has been built on the spot, which is misnamed the Roman Villa Museum (since the building in question was a town house, not a villa). Real villas have been identified and excavated at a number of places. They were well sited and commodious, and combine with all the other evidence about Roman Malta to indicate that the islands enjoyed a quiet prosperity during Republican and early Imperial times. Malta was famous during this time as a centre for the production of fine cloth, excellent sailcloth, and honey (the name Melita, if it does not come from the Phoenician *malat*, port or refuge, was probably derived from the Greek *meli*, honey).

The impression of prosperity and security is not seriously disturbed by the recent discovery that the massive 'round towers' whose ruins are found at various points around the coast, seem to have been erected in the Roman period. Few have yet been properly investigated, but it looks as though they were built near the beginning of Roman rule, when the Punic Wars were still raging and the islands were still an outpost of the developing empire. They could also have been used later during the period of the Civil Wars, or when piracy was rife, but one at least seems to have been converted into a farmhouse by the 1C A.D.

It is probably because it was a prosperous backwater in the centuries that followed the destruction of Carthage that we know so very little about the history of Malta during this period. Shortly after the assassination of Julius Caesar the Sicilians were given Roman citizenship, and presumably the Maltese with them. Otherwise documents are uninformative, and after the 4C A.D., there are no references until A.D. 533, when it is recorded that Belisarius, the general of the Emperor Justinian, called at Malta on his way to the reconquest of Africa from the Vandals. Later, during Justinian's war with Totila, the Byzantine general Artabanes took refuge there from a storm, and it seems clear that at that time the islands were firmly in the possession of the Eastern Roman Empire. The Byzantines once again made them part of the province of Sicily. It is during the Byzantine period that we first hear of a church hierarchy in Malta, though in fact it must have existed much earlier. The Byzantines remained in control until 870 when an Arab fleet appeared and took possession.

The most famous episode in Maltese history during the whole of the Roman period is undoubtedly the shipwreck of St Paul there in either A.D. 58 or 60 when on his way to Rome as a prisoner for trial. The circumstantial description of this event in Ch. XXVII of *Acts*, and of the subsequent welcome of the apostle by Publius, the chief man among the Maltese, whose father he cured of an illness, is vivid and convincing. Small wonder that the tradition is strong in Malta that Paul was able to lay the foundations of a Christian community there during his three month stay. Publius himself, so the story goes, became a bishop, first of Malta and later of Athens. The traditional location of the wreck of Paul's ship is St Paul's island, or Selmunett, on the N.W. side of St Paul's Bay. It has usually been assumed that the house of Publius in which he stayed was at Mdina, but the recent Italian excavations at the site of the 17C church of St Paul Milqi (St Paul Welcomed), which lies not far inland from St Paul's Bay, have revealed that not only was this the site of earlier churches, but also of a Roman villa, which by the 7C A.D. at latest had become a place of pilgrimage which was definitely connected with St Paul.

PREHISTORIC CHRONOLOGY

Period	Phase name*	Approx. date
Neolithic	Għar Dalam	3800 B.C.
	Grey Skorba	3600 B.C.
	Red Skorba	3400 B.C.
Copper Age	Żebbuġ	3200 B.C.
	Mġarr	2900 B.C.
	Ġgantija	2850 B.C.
	Saflieni	2450 B.C.
	Tarxien	2400 B.C.
Bronze Age	Tarxien Cemetery	2000 B.C.
	Borġ in-Nadur	1450 B.C.
	Baħrija	900 B.C.

*adopted from 'type site'

MALTA IN LATER TIMES

Arabs and Normans. Malta's 'Dark Ages' are darker and longer than most, and the island barely emerges again into history before A.D. 870. Then it was conquered by the Abbasid Caliphs, already masters of the greater part of Spain, the s. part of France, Italy, and Sicily. Their influence lingers in the modifications they introduced into the kindred Maltese language, and in the introduction to the island of cotton and citrus fruits. Count Roger of Normandy, after delivering Sicily from the Arabs came in 1090 to the rescue of Malta. The national colours of red and white now embodied in the flag of Malta are supposed to stem from the blazon of the Hauteville family to which he belonged. A few Siculo-Norman palaces survive in Mdina.

The island shared the prosperity of the Sicilian kingdom under their Norman and Hohenstaufen rulers, with Christian and Moslem doubtless living in harmony as in Palermo. The death of Frederick II, the Angevin succession, and expulsion of the Moslems marked the second half of the 13C. After the Sicilian Vespers Charles of Anjou attempted to use Malta as a base from which to recapture Sicily, but was defeated in a naval battle off Valletta. For the next century and a half Malta came under the Aragonese. The institution of the Università, a form of limited local self-government, was often vitiated by the practice of giving the island as a fief to some rapacious governor. In 1428 the Università redeemed the island in perpetuity from enoeffment for a large ransom. The following year the islands were sacked by Barbary corsairs, not the first of many raids the frequency of which increased through the century. Until 1436 there seem to have been only two parishes, Mdina and Birgu, to which the other wayside churches were subordinate. In that year the ten principal settlements were raised to parish status.

The Knights of St John. By a deed of 24 March 1530, still preserved in Maltese archives, the Emp. Charles V made over Malta and its dependencies, in perpetual sovereignty, to the Order of St John of Jerusalem. The Grand Master's sole obligation was the annual presentation on All Saints' Day of a falcon to the Emperor's viceroy in Sicily. The Knights of St John, or Knights Hospitallers, had their origin in a small hospital and chapel inaugurated at Jerusalem for the use of poor and sick pilgrims to the Holy Sepulchre. The hospital, dedicated to St John the Baptist, was founded by merchants of Amalfi with the sanction of the caliph before relations between Christian and moslem had developed into a holy war. The order was thus primarily a nursing brotherhood. The first crusade ended in 1099 with the capture of Jerusalem by Godfrey de Bouillon. In 1113 Paschal II placed the Order and its possessions under papal protection. Its secondary preoccupation with the defence of pilgrims now inevitably became predominant and before long the white cross banner of the Order was spreading terror and dismay among the Saracen armies. Commanderies were formed all over Europe, stimulating zeal and regulating the finances of the Order.

The Knights shared in the great Christian defeat at Tiberias (in which their only English grand master was killed) and Jerusalem was lost to Saladin. In 1191 Richard Coeur de Lion established the Order in Acre, where they remained nearly a hundred years under twelve grand masters. When Acre was taken by the Sultan Khalil, they sought refuge in Cyprus in 1291. In 1310 Fulke de Villaret, after a struggle of four years, seized the island of Rhodes, and established the Order there.

In Rhodes the Knights built a powerful fleet and 'from being hospitallers first and soldiers second became sailors first and hospitallers second'. Pope Clement V assigned to them part of the property of the Templars who had been suppressed in 1312. For two centuries the Knights defied the Turks; they took part in the capture and later in the defence of Smyrna, and withstood two great sieges—in 1444 by the sultan of Egypt and in 1480 by Mehmet II. In June 1522 Suleiman I attacked Rhodes and laid siege to its citadel. Six months later the Knights capitulated on honourable terms. On 1 Jan 1523 Grand Master Villiers de l'Isle Adam, with 180 surviving brethren, left the island. They first retired to Crete and later to Malta.

The Order probably reached its developed form in Rhodes when it comprised three classes, the Knights of Justice, the Chaplains of Obedience, and the Serving Brothers. The military knights, who came to dominate the Order completely, had to prove noble birth without taint of illegitimacy for four generations on both sides of the family, and were thus the most exclusive aristocratic body in Europe. The conventual chaplains, not of necessity nobly born, served the hospital and conventual church. The brothers not only acted as servants but had military duties. For convenience in battle the order was divided into langues, or nationalities. These were eight in number; Auvergne, Provence, France, Aragon, Castile, England, Germany, and Italy. Each langue had its own Auberge, a headquarters building which was the military parallel to its legal equivalent the Inn of Court, with a pilier at its head. Its communal arrangements were not unlike those of a university college. At the head of the Order was a Supreme Council, consisting of the Bishop, the Prior of the conventual church, the Piliers of each langue, the priors, conventual bailiffs, and the Knights Grand Cross. It was presided over by the Grand Master, himself a Knight elected by his brethren.

L'Isle Adam arrived in the autumn and took possession of the fishing village of Birgu on Grand Harbour, leaving the Sicilian aristocracy aloof in Mdina. The fusion of the two traditions was gradual but that a tolerant relationship of all the elements in Malta was established within a generation seems proven by the unity of the defence against the Turks. The galleys of the Knights began to prey again on Moslem shipping and assisted in Philip II's sack of Peñon de la Gomera, a stronghold of the Barbary coast.

Many years passed before the Knights gave up hope of retaking Rhodes or moving elsewhere, an attitude reflected in the small scale of their early building operations in and around Birgu. Though all their military advisers advocated a new fortress on Mt Sceberras, this was not started. A source of revenue was lost when, in 1540, Henry VIII confiscated the forty-three commanderies and preceptories of the Langue of England. In Malta itself the Langue was still deemed to exist and the hope that counter-Reformation would revive it in reality survived for a century. Attacks on Malta and Gozo from the Barbary Coast became increasingly frequent in the 1550s.

In 1565 Suleiman the Magnificent, past his seventieth year, turned the whole strength of the Turkish dominions against his old enemy. The fleet was placed under Admiral Piali, the army under Mustapha Pasha, the two being designated co-commanders of the expedition. One hundred and eighty one ships sailed from the Golden Horn bearing upwards of 30,000 fighting men. The great Corsair Dragut (or Torgud) was to join forces with them. The defenders numbered between 600 and 700 members of the Order with a total force of 8000–9000 men. The Turkish landing was effected unopposed at Marsaxlokk.

Apart from a few cavalry skirmishes the whole campaign quickly resolved itself into the siege and defence of the fortified positions round Grand Harbour. The Turks concentrated first on reducing Fort St Elmo (comp. p. 71), then turned their attention to Senglea and Birgu, the two peninsulas either side of the Port of the Galleys. With a chain across the mouth and a bridge of boats across the water within, this formed one defensible stronghold. Throughout the long summer months all attacks were repulsed until at length the long-awaited and almost-despaired-of relief force from the Sicilian viceroy came to the island's release.

Valletta, founded immediately, quickly gained ascendency over Mdina and the renamed Vittoriosa, a position on which the seal was set when the Bishop of Malta transferred the curia from Mdina in 1622. A serious Turkish attempt to land in 1614 was driven off. The strategy and much of the spending of the 17C was based on the idea of a renewed Turkish threat. Throughout the century forts and look-out towers were built at strategic points on the coast. About 1720 these were supplemented by redoubts and batteries, many of which were later incorporated into the British defence system and so survive to this day. In fact, however, the Turks never recovered at sea from their defeat at Lepanto (1571) and after their rout before Vienna were effectively contained in the Levant and the Balkans by larger European fleets and armies. By the end of the 17C, indeed, the Turks had trading agreements with Christian powers who soon protested against the Order's 'piracies'.

If as a European force the Order slowly declined through obsolescence into anachronism, as the sovereign power in Malta it transformed the island from a poor military base into a flourishing civil state. As military activities declined into privateering, the Order turned more attention to trade. After years of building fortifications and churches Maltese architects turned their hand to warehouses. Malta became a busy centre of entrepôt and transit trade when it was made a relatively cheap port in which to undergo quarantine. It also had a flourishing slave market. The population increased steadily and over the years grouped itself in a decreasing number of larger villages within reach of Grand Harbour. The cotton industry was encouraged to a point where exports of cloth became significant, but economically Malta subsisted on the revenues of its foreign estates and the incomes of the Knights themselves. They, less and less monastic in outlook, made their existence comfortable and even luxurious, a tendency which brought about periodic conflicts with the inquisitor, the bishop, or reforming grand masters.

The Knights' last serious participation in a military expedition against the Porte came in 1715–18 when they assisted the Venetians in their unsuccessful venture off the Peloponnese. The influence of the Knights on diplomacy and even on military decisions was over. As the political power of the Pope, their protector, diminished also, the strategic worth of Malta was increasingly canvassed in various chancelleries. The Order's possessions in France were confiscated during the Revolution, leaving them in financial straits.

On 9 June 1798 Napoleon, convoying 54,000 troops to Egypt, demanded permission to water his ships. When, as expected, this was refused, the islands were taken over with little resistance and the capitulation of Valletta followed. The impregnable fortifications were never put to the test. The Knights were given three days to leave, bearing only their holy relics and personal possessions.

The Order departed never to return and it was left to the Maltese to revolt against the new invader. Not content with looting the treasure of the Knights, the French despoiled the local churches and introduced various anti-clerical measures. A spontaneous uprising in Mdina was sparked off by the French commander's activities after the heartening news had reached Malta of Nelson's victory at the Battle of the Nile. General Vaubois withdrew his garrison of 4000 men behind the defences of Grand Harbour. The Maltese formed a National Assembly and sought British assistance. Nelson placed Capt. Alexander Ball in command of a blockading squadron. Later Ball took civil and military command of the insurgents and was reinforced first by Portuguese marines and later by 1500 British troops under Maj-Gen. Pigot. By the time the French had been starved into surrender in the late summer of 1800, the British were de facto rulers of Malta.

Crown Colony. Proposals to restore the Knights of Malta, under Russian or Neapolitan protection, met with vigorous Maltese opposition. They preferred what they had seen of British protection. British possession of the islands was confirmed by the Treaty of Paris in 1814, by which time the permanent importance of Malta as a naval base was established. As the century advanced the acquisition of more colonies in the E., the operations of the Crimean War, and the opening of the Suez Canal, all increased Britian's dependence on sea power based in the central Mediterranean. Development of commercial facilities was boosted by the opening of the Canal and for a time Grand Harbour shared with Aden the rôle of chief coaling station on the route from Britain to India and the Far East.

Representation of the Maltese people in the affairs of the colony was envisaged from the start and the first constitution was promulgated. in 1835. New constitutions were introduced in 1849, 1887, and 1903, and in 1921 Malta was granted full self-government in all matters of local concern. The system did not work any better than earlier attempts and the constitution, suspended in 1930 and restored in 1932, was again suspended in 1933. Apart from the natural difficulties of an island group which cannot be self-supporting, other perennial problems were the official language controversy (for a long time it was Italian), and the economic difficulty of a civil administration geared to the vicissitudes of military expansion or contraction.

War once again united dissident voices and the second 'Great Siege' with its attendant ordeal by aerial bombardment began while the island was still unprepared. The epic stories of the three Gladiator fighters that in June 1940 took on the Italian air force for three weeks alone, and of the tanker Ohio towed in awash, with sufficient aircraft fuel to stave off inevitable surrender, reflect the more spectacular side of the privations suffered by the Maltese. Lack of food and of fuel, danger, dust, and long hours in underground shelters were the daily lot of everyone. But Malta's rôle was not entirely defensive. Her aircraft late in 1940 played an important part in Wavell's advance on Tripoli. Later her submarine and air attacks against enemy convoys to North Africa not only made supplying Rommel a costly affair but forced the Germans to reinforce Sicily with squadrons needed elsewhere. It was Rommel's successful advance that isolated Malta and made the first six months of 1942 the crucial testing time. The island was awarded its George Cross in April.

In proportion as Montgomery's advance from Alamein gathered momentum, the pressure on Malta lifted, and by the end of the year the invasion of Sicily was being planned from St Angelo and the Phoenicia Hotel. The political armistice between Italy and the Allies was signed aboard H.M.S. Nelson in Grand Harbour after secret military meetings in an olive-grove near Syracuse (Sept. 1943). On his way back from the Teheran conference Franklin D. Roosevelt visited the island and presented a Presidential Citation.

The British Government gave £30 million toward the reconstruction of war damage and in 1947 restored internal self-government. The idea of integrating Malta with the United Kingdom foundered on the problem of social security contribution as much as on religious difficulties. After a strained period when in 1959 the constitution was again suspended, Malta became independent in September 1964. Elizabeth II at the islanders' request assumed the additional style of Queen of Malta.

GRAND MASTERS OF THE ORDER OF ST. JOHN IN MALTA

(1521)1530–1534　Philippe Villiers de L'Isle Adam (*French*)
1534–1535　Pietro del Ponte (*Italian*)
1535–1536　Didier de Saint Jaille (*French*)
1536–1553　Juan de Homedes (*Spanish*)
1553–1557　Claude de la Sengle (*French*)
1557–1568　Jean Parisot de la Vallette (*French*)
1568–1572　Pietro del Monte (*Italian*)
1572–1581　Jean l'Evêque de la Cassière (*French*)
1581–1595　Hugues Loubenx de Verdalle (*French*)
1595–1601　Martin Garzes (*Spanish*)
1601–1622　Alof de Wignacourt (*French*)
1622–1623　Luiz Mendez de Vasconcellos (*Portuguese*)
1623–1636　Antoine de Paule (*French*)
1636–1657　Jean Paul de Lascaris Castellar (*French*)
1657–1660　Martin de Redin (*Spanish*)
　　　1660　Annet de Clermont de Chattes Gessan (*French*)
1660–1663　Rafael Cotoner (*Spanish*)
1663–1680　Nicolas Cotoner (*Spanish*)
1680–1690　Gregorio Carafa (*Italian*)
1690–1697　Adrien de Wignacourt (*French*)
1697–1720　Ramón Perellos y Roccaful (*Spanish*)
1720–1722　Marc'Antonio Zondadari (*Italian*)
1722–1736　Antonio Manoel de Vilhena (*Portuguese*)
1736–1741　Ramón Despuig (*Spanish*)
1741–1773　Manoel Pinto de Fonseca (*Portuguese*)
1773–1775　Francisco Ximenes de Texada (*Spanish*)
1775–1797　Emmanuel de Rohan Polduc (*French*)
1797–1798　Ferdinand von Hompsech (*German*)

The possible variants of medieval spelling are numerous and unimportant.

REPRESENTATIVES OF THE CROWN AT MALTA
CIVIL COMMISSIONERS

1799–1801	Captain Alexander Ball, R.N., President of the Provisional Government
1801	Major-General Henry Pigot, in charge of the troops and of the Government
1801–1802	Sir Charles Cameron
1802–1809	Rear-Admiral Sir Alexander Ball, Bart.
1810–1813	Lieutenant-General Sir Hildebrand Oakes.

GOVERNORS

1813–1824	Lieutenant-General The Hon. Sir Thomas Maitland
1824–1826	General the Marquess of Hastings
1827–1836	Major General the Hon. Sir Frederic Ponsomby
1836–1843	Lieutenant-General Sir Henry Bouverie
1843–1847	Lieutenant-General Sir Patrick Stuart
1847–1851	The Right Hon. Richard More O'Ferrall
1851–1858	Major General Sir William Reid
1858–1864	Lieutenant-General Sir John Gaspard le Marchant
1864–1867	Lieutenant-General Sir Henry Storks
1867–1872	General Sir Patrick Grant
1872–1878	General Sir Charles Van Straubenzee
1878–1884	General Sir Arthur Borton
1884–1888	General Sir Lintern Simmonds
1888–1890	Lieutenant-General Sir Henry Torrens
1890–1893	Lieutenant-General Sir Henry Smyth
1893–1899	General Sir Arthur Fremantle
1899–1903	Lieutenant-General Lord Grenfell
1903–1907	General Sir Mansfield Clarke, Bart.
1907–1909	Lieutenant-General Sir Henry Grant
1909–1915	General Sir Leslie Rundle
1915–1919	Field-Marshal Lord Methuen
1919–1924	Field-Marshal Viscount Plumer
1924–1927	General Sir Walter N. Congreve, V.C.
1927–1931	General Sir John du Cane
1931–1936	General Sir David Campbell
1936–1940	General Sir Charles Bonham-Carter
1940–1942	Lieutenant-General Sir William Dobbie
1942–1944	Field-Marshal Viscount Gort, V.C.
1944–1946	Lieutenant-General Sir Edmond Schrieber
1946–1949	Sir Francis (later Lord) Douglas
1949–1954	Sir Gerald Creasy
1954–1959	Major General Sir Robert Laycock
1959–1962	Admiral Sir Guy Grantham
1962–1964	Sir Maurice Dorman

GOVERNORS-GENERAL

1964–	Sir Maurice Dorman

PRIME MINISTERS OF MALTA

1921–1923	Hon. Joseph Howard, O.B.E.
1923–1924	Hon. Francesco Buhagiar
1924–1927	Hon. Sir Ugo P. Mifsud, K.B.
1927–1932	Hon. Sir Gerald Strickland, G.C.M.G. (Lord Strickland)
1932–1933	Sir Ugo P. Mifsud, K.B.
1947–1950	Hon. Dr (later Sir) Paul Boffa, O.B.E.
1950 (Sept–Dec)	Hon. Dr Enrico Mizzi
1950–1955	Hon. Dr Giorgio Borg Olivier, LL.D.
1955–1958	Hon. Dom. Mintoff, M.A. (Oxon.)
1962–	Hon, Dr Giorgio Borg Olivier, LL.D.

PRACTICAL INFORMATION

APPROACHES TO MALTA

MALTA can be reached by air directly from England; by air or sea from Italy, from Sicily, or from Tripoli. Passengers from Europe will make their best air connection in Rome (Alitalia). In the summer months there is communication with Sardinia. Few other regular services exist, though it is possible occasionally to take ship from London or from Cyprus.

From England the direct air service takes 3–4 hours; by any combination of overland routes via Italy it is difficult to complete the journey in less than 2½–3 days and several changes of train are necessary. The cost of the journey overland (if meals and the inevitable expenses of transfer from rail to ship are taken into account) will be considerably greater than the excursion return air fare.

Travellers who wish to save the bother of making their own reservations will be advised to do so through a **Travel Agent,** choosing a reputable member of the British Association of Travel Agents.

These organizations, for a small fee, obtain travel tickets, make hotel reservations, deal with the problems of foreign currency, and, if desired, arrange tours for individuals or parties. A selection of agents in London is given below; several of them have branches in other towns.

Thomas Cook & Son, 45 Berkeley St., W.1, and many branches; *American Express*, 6 Haymarket, S.W.1, 89 Mount St., W.1; *Dean & Dawson*, 81 Piccadilly, W.1, etc.; *Frames' Tours*, 25 Tavistock Place, W.C.1, 42 Albemarle St., W.1, 80 Southampton Row, W.C.1, etc.; *Global Tours*, 318 High Holborn, W.C1, 191 Regent St., W.1, etc.; *Poly Travel Ltd*, 311 Regent St., W.1, 73 Oxford St., W.1, etc.

Travellers who enjoy planning their own journey cannot do better than consult the Malta Government Tourist Office, 24 Haymarket, London, S.W.1, for general information. They can then work out their schedules with the aid of the time-tables listed below and purchase tickets at the relevant addresses given.

TIMETABLES. *Cook's Continental Timetable* (monthly; 10/6) is the leading international timetable. The *A.B.C. World Airways Guide* (monthly; 30/–) is the most comprehensive air travel guide published in England.

Air Services between London (etc.) and Malta (Luqa) are maintained by British European Airways (B.E.A.) in association with Malta Airlines. Full information may be obtained from *B.E.A*

Dorland Hall, Lower Regent St., S.W.1. Service frequencies in 1968 are as follows: From LONDON (Heathrow) direct at least twice daily; 3–7 times weekly via *Naples*; twice weekly via *Palermo*; weekly in summer via *Alghero* (Sardinia). Also from BIRMINGHAM direct weekly in summer; from MANCHESTER direct, once or twice weekly. Cheapest return fare in 1968, £37/10.

By Sea there is no scheduled service, but a limited number of passengers is carried by the Prince Line on a service at irregular intervals between London and Haifa, which calls at Malta, Limassol and Famagusta. Details of sailing from 58 Leadenhall St., London, E.C.3. Single fare to Malta in 1968, £50–£58.

By Rail and Sea. The *British Rail Travel Centre*, Rex House, Lower Regent St., London, S.W.1, provides travel tickets, sleeping berth tickets, seat reservations, etc., on Continental (as well as British) transport services.

The *Società di Navigazione Tirrenia* operates three services to Malta:

Line 10 from Naples via Malta to Tripoli, every ten days.

Line 11 from Naples via Malta to Benghazi, every ten days (cars carried).

Line 19 from Syracuse to Malta, three times weekly (overnight sailing).

Details of these services may be obtained from 35 St James's St., S.W.1.

Motoring. Cars may be hired simply and cheaply in Malta (see below) where the rule of the road is the same as in the United Kingdom. Extra care is needed since local driving is often erratic and overtaking on the left frequent; officially there is a speed limit of 25 m.p.h. in built-up areas and 40 m.p.h. everywhere else. British drivers taking their own cars by any of the multitudinous routes across France, Belgium, Luxembourg, Switzerland, and Italy need only the vehicle registration book, a valid national driving licence (with a translation of its provisions into Italian; or an international driving permit), and an International Insurance Certificate (the 'Green Card'). A nationality plate (e.g. GB) must be affixed to the rear of the vehicle so as to be illuminated by the tail lamp.

The continental rule of the road is to drive on the right and overtake on the left. The provisions of the respective highway codes in the countries of transit, though similar, have important variations, especially with regard to priority, speed limits, and pedestrian crossings. Membership of the *Automobile Association* (Fanum House, Leicester Square, London, W.C.2), the *Royal Automobile Club* (83 Pall Mall, S.W.1), or the *Royal Scottish Automobile Club* entitles motorists to many of the facilities of affiliated societies on the Content and may save trouble and anxiety. The U.K. motoring organizations are represented at most of the

sea and air ports, both at home and on the Continent, to assist
their members with customs formalities.

Car Ferries are operated by British and French Railways from
Dover to Calais, Boulogne, and Dunkirk and from Newhaven to
Dieppe; also by Townsend Ferries from Dover to Calais; by
Thoresen Ferries from Southampton to Le Havre and Cherbourg;
by British Rail and Zeeland Steamship Co. from Harwich to Hook
of Holland; by Belgian State Marine from Harwich to Ostend
and from both Dover and Folkestone to Ostend; and by Normandy
Ferries from Rosslare (Ireland) to Le Havre. A hovercraft service
starts in 1968 from Ramsgate to Calais. In London full particulars
are available from the A.A., R.A.C., or British Rail, all at the
Continental Car Ferry Centre, 52 Grosvenor Gardens, S.W.1.

The Tirrenia service from Syracuse to Malta (see above) has
drive-on car-carrying facilities.

Air Ferries for cars are run by *British United Air Ferries* (Portland
House, Victoria, London, S.W.1) from Southend, Lydd, or
Coventry to Calais, Le Touquet, Ostend, Rotterdam, etc.

PETROL in Malta is sold by the gallon at a cost of 4/1–4/6.

Passports. Citizens of the United Kingdom and Italy require only
a valid passport or an Identity Card to enter Malta for a visit not
exceeding three months.

Citizens of Commonwealth Countries, Austria, Belgium, Den-
mark, Eire, Federal Republic of Germany, Finland, France, Greece,
Leichtenstein, Luxembourg, Monaco, Netherlands, Norway,
Portugal, Spain, Sweden, Switzerland, Turkey, United States of
America and Uruguay require only a passport for a visit not
exceeding three months. Visitors wishing to stay over three months
are required to apply to the Administrative Secretary, Office of the
Prime Minister, Immigration Branch, St John's Square, Valletta.

Visitors not mentioned above require a visa, application for
which should be made through a British Consular Office.

Custom House. Personal clothing, personal belongings and house-
hold effects are not liable for duty if used. Cigars, cigarettes and
tobacco (in reasonable quantities) are allowed free but are cheaper
in Malta than in the United Kingdom.

Returning travellers may be reminded that all articles purchased
abroad are now dutiable or forbidden in Britain, special attention
being paid to watches and cameras, but a limited amount of new
personal clothing, 200 cigarettes or $\frac{1}{2}$ lb. of tobacco, a bottle of
wine and a bottle of spirits, a small bottle of perfume, and souvenirs
to the value of £5 are usually passed free, if declared. Foreign
reprints of copyright English books may be confiscated.

Currency Regulations. Malta is in the sterling area and citizens
of the United Kingdom may take there unlimited credit facilities
(letter of credit, bank transfer, travellers' cheques, etc.). In sterling
notes not more than £10 (plus £5 in silver) may be taken out of

Great Britain by British or American travellers. Money for transit facilities overland is subject to the foreign currency provisions in force (in 1968 £50 per person, plus an allowance of £25 for a car).

There are no local restrictions on the amounts of currency which may be brought into Malta in currency notes, travellers' cheques or letters of credit.

Travellers leaving Malta after a temporary visit may take out:
Sterling notes and/or Maltese currency notes to a total of £25; Travellers' cheques, letters of credit, etc., brought in by them or issued to them by authorized dealers; notes expressed in foreign currencies up to the equivalent of £250 or the amount brought by them into Malta, whichever is the greater.

Money. Silver and copper coins are the same as in the United Kingdom; the five-pound, pound and ten shillings notes are Maltese but of the same value.

Arrival in Malta by air. Passengers are taken by bus (3/6 single) to the Phoenicia Hotel terminal at Floriana, but many of the larger hotels meet scheduled aircraft with their own transport or by taxi. Arrangements to be met should be confirmed in advance through the agent or the hotel.

HOTELS AND RESTAURANTS

Hotels. There are upwards of fifty hotels in Malta, more than half of which are situated in Sliema and St Julian's, about half-a-dozen in Gozo, and two on Comino. These are all listed with details of their amenities in a leaflet obtainable free from the Malta Government Tourist Office. A selection is mentioned topographically in the text, but no derogatory judgement should be implied by any omissions. New hotels are in construction at intervals round the coast. There are none in the Three Cities, or indeed anywhere in the part of the island E. of Valletta.

Daily terms vary between 15/– and £6 for bed and breakfast and between 25/– and £10 for full board, accommodation in Gozo being at the cheaper end of the scale.

Furnished flats, houses and villas are available at rents varying between £25 and £40 per fortnight according to locality and degree of accommodation and amenities provided. Cheaper rates are available for long leases.

A list of travel agents who provide furnished accommodation is issued by the Tourist Board.

Restaurants. With a few exceptions in Valletta, restaurants are open only for dinner, though lunch can be obtained by non-residents at most hotels. Many establishments out of town have dinner-dances.

LICENSING HOURS. Opening hours of bars, restaurants and cafés normally extend between 9 a.m. and 1 a.m. Alcoholic beverages may be bought at a time these establishments are open. Local wines and locally brewed beers are cheap and spirits relatively cheap. Most hotel bars close between 1 p.m. and 4 p.m. and some open after 6 p.m.

Food in Maltese restaurants tends to a somewhat depressing compromise between traditional English, usually prepared from inadequate ingredients, and southern Italian. Local specialities include some tasty dishes among which the following will be frequently encountered:

Minestra, a village vegetable soup akin to minestrone.

Timpana, macaroni with liver, soft and hard boiled eggs, onions, and aubergines, baked in pastry.

Torta tal-Lampuki (lampuki pie), made from a local fish (lampuka). Slices of fish are fried and covered with pastry, then baked with tomatoes, onions, parsley, peas, and cauliflower.

Bringiel fil-forn, stuffed aubergines.

Ross fil-forn, baked rice with minced meat and eggs.

Qarnita, octopus or cuttle-fish with olives, onions, raisins, nuts, and peas, stewed in wine.

Bragioli (beef olives), minced meat, eggs, bacon, breadcrumbs, parsley and olives, wrapped in a thin roll of steak.

Hut biz-zalza, tunny with capers and tomato sauce.

Wines of local vintage are cheap and palatable. Among them may be mentioned *Marsovin Special Reserve*, a full red wine akin to the heavier reds of Italy such as Barolo, Alberobello, etc.; *Verdala Rosé Classico*; and *Lachrima Vitis*. The Gozitan wines are particularly strong.

TRANSPORT

Buses run from Valletta/Floriana to all parts of the island of Malta, and from Victoria rather less frequently to most villages in Gozo. Each route is differentiated not by number but by the colour of the bus. At main boarding points in Valletta, Floriana, Sliema, etc. it is usual to buy a ticket at the appropriate kiosk; passengers from intermediate points pay the conductor. Fares, which are very cheap, are increased slightly at night and on Sundays. Tickets are inspected frequently.

In addition to the services radiating from Valletta/Floriana listed on p. 53, there are three cross-country routes:

Birkirkara–Sliema (green with red band),

Rabat–St Paul's Bay (dark blue).

Cospicua–Xghajra (light red with blue band).

Post-Buses to Gozo, see Rte 11.

Taxis are identified by red number-plates, with white numbers preceded by the word 'Taxi' also in white. Taxis, which are all fitted with taxi-meters, charge Government controlled prices. A number of car-hire firms offer self-drive cars comprehensively insured. Among them are:

Gzira Garage, Reid St., Gzira.

Hertz, 19 St Anthony St., Sliema.

Texas Garage, 305 D'Argens Road, Gzira.

The hire charge is approximately £2 per day, the hirer buying his own petrol. Where necessary International Driving Permits and other driving licences are endorsed free to *bona fide* tourists at Police Headquarters (Floriana).

KARROZZIN, or horse-drawn victorias, are available for sight-seeing hire.

Sight-seeing Tours are arranged by local agencies and pick up passengers at about 9.15 and 2.15 from their hotels.

POSTAL AND OTHER SERVICES

The General Post Office is in Merchants Street, Valletta. Other towns and most villages have offices and there are also sub-offices and agencies where stamps may be bought in Valletta and Sliema. The main Parcel Post Office is in Victory Square, Valletta.

Letters ($\frac{1}{2}$ oz.) to the United Kingdom go by airmail daily at the standard rate (4d). Local postage is 2d for the first oz.

TELEPHONE. Local calls are on an automatic dialling system and call-box facilities are available. Malta has telephonic communication with most countries of the world and transferred-charge calls are accepted to the United Kingdom. The charge to the United Kingdom is 30/- for 3 minutes.

TELEGRAMS. Cable & Wireless operate a 24 hour service from Mercury House, St George's and from St John's Square, Valletta.

AMUSEMENTS

Theatres and Cinemas. Plays, concerts, shows and operas are mainly held in the historic Manoel Theatre in Valletta between October and April. During the summer season (May–September) these are held in the open-air.

There are upwards of forty cinemas in the Island, where British, American and Italian films are shown.

Sports. The *United Services Sports Club* at Marsa (temp. membership 10/- per week) affords facilities for playing tennis, squash, badminton, etc. and golf at the *Royal Malta Golf Club*. HORSE RACING at Marsa Racecourse on Sun aft. at 2 in late-Oct to mid-May. POLO, also at Marsa, on Saturdays.

Water Sports. SAILING: the *Royal Malta Yacht Club*, Hay Wharf, Marsamxett, organizes races on Wed and Sat in Apr–Nov and on Sundays, including an annual race to Sicily. WATER-SKIING in Valletta, St George's, St Paul's and Mellieħa Bays. FISHING: tuna, swordfish and shark can be caught in the seas around the islands. No licence is required for fishing from the shore with rod and line.

Swimming. Much of the Maltese coastline falls sheer into deep water but there are no tides and few currents. The sea temperature in summer averages 74°F and reaches 82°. Sandy beaches occur in the N.W. near Mellieħa at Ġnejna Bay, Għain Tuffieħa Bay, Golden Bay, Anchor Bay, Paradise Bay, Armier Bay, and Għadira (Mellieħa Bay). Rock bathing is good at Sliema, in St Paul's Bay, off the Delimara peninsula (Peter's Pool), and in St Thomas Bay. Beach establishments are open between May and October and are equipped with the usual facilities. Għar Lapsi and Wied iż-Żurrieq are frequented for underwater fishing. Bathing is especially good on Comino. In Gozo Marsalforn, Xlendi, and Ramla Bay are the most popular beaches. Two-piece bathing costumes ('bikinis') are not permitted anywhere.

The Lido at the Dragonara Palace is open in June–Oct (10–6.30) and the pools at the Villa Rosa Beach Club (St George's Bay) and the Plevna Hotel (Sliema) are open to the public. Many other hotels have their own pools.

GENERAL HINTS

Season. The mean figures in the table below give a fair general picture of the pattern of the Maltese climate. April, May, early June, and October are probably the best months for an active visit, July and August being too warm for comfort. January is the least pleasant month and may indeed be as cold as London, though very much brighter. The day to day sequences, especially in winter, can be nearly as variable as those suffered by the British Isles. In summer it is generally fine and warm with pleasant N.W. breezes and virtually no rain. Occasionally, however, crops are withered and tempers frayed by the *xlokk*, or sirocco, which blows from the Sahara raising the humidity uncomfortably. In September storms may presage the warm but showery months of October and November. The long winter hours of sunshine are punctuated by depressions when their warmth is dissipated by strong winds: the *majjistral* from the N.W.; the *tramuntana* from the N.; or the *grigal* from the N.E. Though frost is virtually unknown, hailstones and flurries of snow are not. Gales are sometimes severe. Rainfall, though averaging c. 20 in. per year, can vary widely between years of drought with only 10 in. and of flood with as much as 40 inches.

Month	Average Sunshine hours	Rainfall ins. mm	Average Max. F C	Temperature Min. F C
Jan	5.2	3.26 – 83.5	63 17.2	46 7.8
Feb	5.1	2.17 – 55.6	64 17.8	47 8.3
Mar	6.9	1.58 – 40.5	68 20.0	48 8.9
Apr	8.5	0.87 – 22.3	72 22.2	51 10.6
May	10.2	0.41 – 10.5	78 25.6	56 13.3
June	11.7	0.08 – 2.0	85 29.4	63 17.2
July	12.6	0.02 – 0.5	92 33.3	69 20.6
Aug	11.9	0.22 – 5.6	91 32.8	70 21.1
Sep	9.1	1.19 – 30.5	86 30.0	69 20.6
Oct	7.1	3.25 – 83.3	82 27.8	63 17.2
Nov	5.9	3.30 – 86.9	74 23.3	54 12.2
Dec	5.1	3.81 – 97.7	67 19.4	49 9.4

TIME. Malta uses Central European Time which is the same as British Standard Time.

Health. The climate is generally healthy, and no inoculations or vaccination are necessary. Exceptionally in high summer sand-flies blown over from Africa can bring their particularly unpleasant fever. This is conveyed by a bite; the onset is sudden and violent but not dangerous. A District Medical Officer is on duty in every village. Tap water is safe but not very palatable. Fresh fruit should be washed.

Expenses. Hotel prices have risen steeply in the last few years, and are now comparable with those in the British Isles. Drinks are cheap, especially local wines. Transport (bus and ferry services) is very cheap.

Language. English is almost universally spoken. The only acquaintance the visitor need have with Maltese is sufficient ability to pronounce place-names. Maltese, a Semitic language supposedly Phoenician in origin, had been modified by later Arabic accretions before A.D. 1000. Many of the words added to the language in our millennium are of European origin, mainly from Italian or English, both of which languages have been widely understood and practised in the islands. Maltese is written in modified western characters. The alphabet has 29 letters: a b ċ d e f ġ g għ h ħ i j k l m n o p q r s t u v w x z ż. The vowel sounds are pure as in Italian, except that ie (as in Sliema) is a true diphthong. The following consonants have approximately the same pronunciation as in English: b d f k l m n p r t v. Ċ has the sound of ch in church; ġ as English g in George (spelled Ġorġ in Maltese); g as English g in go; għ is generally silent; ħ has a harder sound than h, but the two are not normally differentiable to an English ear; j as y in yet; q is virtually a glottal stop, comparable with the lack of sound accorded by a Cockney to the final t in that, or with the catch called the stød in Danish; s is always sibilant as in say; w as English w in wet; x as sh in shine; z has the sound of ts in cats or the German z in zehn, while ż is like English z in zebra.

The 24 Maltese consonants are divided into 'moon' letters (b f ġ g għ h ħ j k m p q v w) and 'sunny' letters (ċ d l n r s t x z ż). Il, meaning the, retains its form before a moon letter, but modifies the l to the first letter of any noun beginning with a sunny letter. Ta' (of) becomes Tal (of the) by contraction and is equally subject to change, e.g.

Il-Knisja tal-Madonna ta' Fatima, Our Lady of Fatima Church
but, Iċ-Ċimiterju tad-Duluri, Our Lady of Sorrows Cemetery.
Hal (meaning village) modifies similarly.

Place Names. Since Malta achieved independence a 'pure' Maltese spelling has prevailed over the Italianate equivalents seen in most old maps. Place-names in this book follow the latest maps produced in 1962–63 by the Directorate of Overseas Surveys, though variants are given where they are still widely in use. Names of streets are displayed bilingually in Malta and are given here in the English version as recorded in Baron Sceberras D'Amico Inguanez's admirable Street Guide (comp. p. 48).

Public Holidays. The chief public holidays are New Year's Day; 6 Jan (Epiphany); 13 Feb (St Paul's Shipwreck); 19 Mar (St Joseph); Good Friday; 1 May (St Joseph the Worker); Ascension Day; Corpus Christi; 29 June (SS Peter & Paul); 15 Aug (Assumption); 8 Sept (National Day); 21 Sept (Independence Day); 1 Nov (All Saints); 8 Dec (Immaculate Conception); Christmas Day.

Shopping Hours. All business establishments are generally open between the hours of 9 a.m. and 8 p.m. with a 2-hour lunch break. They are closed on Sundays. BANKS are open Mon to Fri, 8.30–12.30; Sat 8.30–12.

Festivals. *Carnival* is celebrated with colourful festivity in Valletta the week before Lent. Passion processions in costume are held on *Good Friday*. The *Mnarja*, a traditional festival of music, singing, and dancing is held in the streets of Mdina (with horse and donkey racing) on 28–29 June. A *Regatta* in Grand Harbour commemorates the victory of 1565 every 8 September. *National Day* is marked on 21 September by bands, music and fireworks in Valletta.

Festas. Every parish has an annual day of festival determined by its patron saint, but not necessarily celebrated on that saint's day. Rabat has two. Celebrations include *Fireworks*, which are usually on the Saturday evening if the festa is celebrated on the

Sunday. The following calendar gives the normal dates or movable feasts of celebrations for the 48 parishes of Malta:

Last Sun in Jan	Safi
10 Feb	Valletta (St Paul's)
Second Sun after Easter	Floriana
Fourth Sun after Easter	Balzan
Fifth Sun after Easter	Tarxien
Sun after 8 May	Marsaxlokk
Sun after 12 May	Żebbug
Sun after Ascension Day	Qormi (St George's)
Trinity Sunday	Marsa
Corpus Christi	Rabat
Last Sun in May	Sliema (St Gregory's)
First Sun in June	Żurrieq
Fourth Sun after Whitsun	Sliema (Sacred Heart)
Third Sun in June	Siġġiewi
Sunday after 29 June	Rabat
Second Sunday in July	Gżira, Kalkara, Qormi (St Sebastian's)
Third Sun in July	Mdina
Sun after 16 July	Msida
Fourth Sun in July	Paola
Sun after 26 July	Santa Venera
Last Sun in July	St Paul's Bay
First Sun in Aug	Birżebbuġa
4 Aug	Valletta (St Dominic's)
6 Aug	Lija
Sun after 7 Aug	Hamrun
10 Aug	Vittoriosa
15 Aug	Attard, Għaxaq, Gudja, Mosta, Qrendi
Sun after 15 Aug	Dingli, Marsaskala, Mġarr, Mqabba
18 Aug	Birkirkara
Third Sun in Aug	Sliema (Stella Maris)
24 Aug	Għargħur
Last Sun in Aug	St Julian's
8 Sept	Mellieħa, Naxxar, Senglea
Sun after 8 Sept	Żabbar
Second Sun in Nov	Kirkop
25 Nov	Żejtun
30 Nov	Luqa
8 Dec	Cospicua

In Gozo the thirteen parishes celebrate as follows:

Corpus Christi	Għasri
Ten days after Corpus Christi	Victoria (Fontana)
Nearest Sun to 24 June	Xewkija
29 June	Nadur
Sun after 2 July	Għarb
Second Sun in July	Kerċem
Third Sun in July	Victoria (St George's)
Fourth Sun in July	Sannat
First Sun in August	Qala
10 Aug	San Lawrenz
Sun after 15 Aug	Żebbug
8 Sept	Xagħra
Third Sun in Sept	Għainsielem

Museums and Archaeological Sites under the control of the Museum Department are open as follows:

16 June–30 Sept	8.30–1.30.
1 Oct–15 June	Malta: 8.30–1, 2–4.30.
	Gozo: 8.30–12, 1–4.30.

All are closed on Public Holidays; and on Gozo also on Tues in winter. Admission to single sites is 1/- (to those in Valletta 2/-), but at any site a comprehensive ticket (2/-) can be bought which is valid for all for one day only.

The following are the sites concerned:

Valletta: National Museum, Armoury; Vittoriosa, Inquisitor's Palace; Hal Saflieni Hypogeum; Tarxien, Temples; Ħaġar Qim and Mnajdra temples; Għar Dalam; Rabat: Roman Museum, St Paul's Catacombs; Victoria, Citadel Museum; Xagħra, Ġgantija temples.

Details of other admission times and fees will be found in the appropriate place in the text.

CHURCHES. The Roman Catholic authorities are strict about dress in church. Women must cover arms, head, and shoulders; men must not wear shorts or have bare upper arms.

BOOKS AND MAPS

The Maltese archives are extensive and much detailed work based on them has been published in Malta. The list here given is concerned in the main with more general works that are relatively obtainable in the United Kingdom.

Recent general introductions to the Maltese scene include *Luke, Sir Harry*: 'Malta' (2nd edn, 1960); *Bryans, Robin*: 'Malta and Gozo' (1966); *Hogg, Garry*: 'Malta: blue-water island' (1967); *Brockman, Eric*: 'Last Bastion' (1961); *Kininmonth, Christopher*: 'The Brass Dolphins' (1957). *Ryan, F. W.*: 'Malta' (1910) is interesting for its account of bygone customs.

For Maltese prehistory the essentials are *Zammit, Sir Themistocles*: 'Prehistoric Malta: the Tarxien temple' (1930); *Evans, John D.*: 'Malta' (1959); and *Trump, D. H.*: 'Skorba' (1966); also the articles by the two last and *Bernabó Brea* in *Antiquity* vols. 34–37 (1960–63). These should all be read in the light of the introductory essay in the Blue Guide.

HISTORY. By far the best general survey is *Blouet, Brian*: 'The story of Malta' (1967), with a very well selected bibliography for further reading. The latest and most readable account of the Great Siege is *Bradford, Ernle*: 'The Great Siege; Malta 1565' (1961), based very largely on the eye-witness account of *Fr. Balbi di Correggio*, the original Spanish MS. of which is available in English in two translations both entitled 'The Siege of Malta', by *Bradford* (Folio Soc. 1965) and by *H. A. Balbi* (Copenhagen, 1961). For the history of the Order *Schermahorn, Elizabeth*: 'Malta of the Knights' (1929) may be supplemented by *Engel, Claire Eliane*: 'Knights of Malta: a gallery of portraits' (1963). Much further information may be found in *Cassar, P.*: 'A Medical History of Malta' (1965). *Hardman, William*: 'A History of Malta during the period of the French and British Occupations, 1798–1815' (1909) is a detailed study, but works on the later 19C in Malta are less easily consulted. They include *Laferla, A. V.*: 'British Malta' (Malta, 1947).

Of innumerable books on aspects of the Second World War may be mentioned: '*Bartimeus*': 'The Epic of Malta' (1943), propagandist but graphically illustrated by official photographs; *Lloyd, Sir Hugh*: 'Briefed to Attack' (1949); *Cunningham of Hyndhope, Viscount*: 'A Sailor's Odyssey' (1951); *Shankland, Peter and Hunter, A.*: 'Malta Convoy' (1961); *Gilchrist, R. T.*: 'Malta Strikes Back' (1945).

ART. *Hughes, J. Quentin*: 'The Building of Malta, 1530–1795' (1956) surveys the architecture of the Order in detail, but omits Gozo. There is no generally available equivalent for the Colonial period. *Sammut, Dr Edward*: 'Art in Malta' (Malta, 1954) is more important than its size would indicate, and the same author's short guides to 'The Co-Cathedral of St John' (1950); 'The Palace of the Grand Masters' (1951); and 'The Monuments of Mdina' (1960) are equally valuable.

In Malta the most comprehensive sources of ephemeral practical information are *Hilary, B. (ed.)*: 'The Malta Year Book' (Malta, St Julian's, annually); 'Coming Events in Malta' (Malta Govt Tourist Office, weekly).

Maps. Essential to motorists and walkers alike are the excellent maps at 1 : 25,000 (c. 2½ in. to the mile) published (1962–63) by the Directorate of Overseas Surveys. Malta occupies two sheets and Gozo (with Comino) one. These are readily available in London from Messrs Stanford's of Long Acre, W.C.2, or from bookshops in Malta. For detailed exploration of the villages the 'Malta Street Guide' (1958) by *Baron Sceberras D'Amico Inguanez* is invaluable.

EXPLANATIONS

TYPE. The main routes are described in large type. Smaller type is used for branch-routes and excursions, for historical and preliminary paragraphs, and (generally speaking) for descriptions of greater detail or minor importance.

ASTERISKS indicate points of special interest or excellence.

DISTANCES are given in miles cumulatively from the starting-point of the route or sub-route.—HEIGHTS are given in English feet.

POPULATIONS are given to the nearest fifty according to the official estimates of 1965.

ABBREVIATIONS. In addition to generally accepted and self-explanatory abbreviations, the following occur in the Guide:

Adm.	admission	m.	mile(s)
Bp.	bishop	Mons.	Monseigneur
C	century	r.	right
c.	circa	Rte	route
Card.	cardinal	St	Saint
G.M.	grand master	St.	street
l.	left		

Italo-Maltese Christian names:

Ant.	Antonio	Gius.	Giuseppe
Dom.	Domenico	Lor.	Lorenzo
Fil.	Filippo	Nic.	Nicolo
Franc.	Francesco	Stef.	Stefano
Gerol.	Gerolamo	Vinc.	Vincenzo
Giov.	Giovanni	Vitt.	Vittorio

MALTA

The **Maltese Islands,** forming since 1964 an independent sovereign
state of the British Commonwealth, are a group of five islands
centrally situated in the Mediterranean. They are distant 58 m.
from Cape Passero in Sicily and c. 180 m. from Cape Bon near
Tunis. Gibraltar lies 1141 m. to the w. and Alexandria 944 m. to the
E. Between *Malta* itself, the principal island (95 sq. m.), and its
smaller sister, *Gozo* (26 sq. m.), lies *Comino* (1 sq. m.); the remaining islets, *Cominotto* and *Filfla*, are uninhabited and of no
importance. The total population of 316,450 is divided very un-
equally between Malta with 291,250 inhab. and Gozo with 25,200
of whom under thirty reside in Comino. The urban areas of the
main island thus have a density of population hardly equalled in
Europe. The capital, Valletta, on the N.E. coast of Malta, is situated
in lat. 35° 53′ N.; long. 14° 32′ E.

Nowhere higher than 850 ft, the island of Malta is geologically
composed of sedimentary limestone with deposits of greensand and
blue clay, and despite the proximity of seismic areas to the N. and
w. is nowhere volcanic. The succession from the lowest stratum to
the top is Lower Coralline limestone, Globigerina limestone, blue
clay, greensand, and Upper Coralline limestone. In general the
surface is flat, rising gradually towards the w. coast. The N.W.,
shattered by a series of faults, consists of bare limestone ridges and
fertile depressions. There are no rivers and the rocky wieds are
generally dry except during periods of heavy rain. With a low
rainfall, there are few perennial springs and most domestic water is
drawn from wells. About half of the surface is covered with a thin
rich mould which proves surprisingly fertile since the island's
small rainfall is restricted almost entirely to four winter months with
long periods of drought in summer. Save for orchards of citrus
fruits, carobs, figs, and olives, there are few trees. The principal
danger is of soil erosion, especially during the frequent gales, and
the island is everywhere criss-crossed with protective stone walls.
These and the ubiquitous prickly pear leave an impression of
barrenness, belied in April by the orange blossom and the crimson
fields of silla, a clover grown for fodder. For the geology of Gozo
and its consequences see p. 113.

The prosperity of the islands depended almost entirely for a
century and a half on their importance to Britain as a naval and
military base. In many obvious ways English influences have
penetrated the Maltese way of life; they are not thought of as alien
or to be shed with Independence. Indeed what has disappeared
recently has rather been the faldetta, the traditional female headgear

Malta

⊟ Tower ◼ Modern Fort ⊡ Redoubt
✶ Antiquity ⚓ Church

0   1   2   3 Miles
0   1   2   3   4   5 Kilometres

St Catherine Bay
St George's Bay
St Julian's Bay
St Julian's Point

St Julian's
Sliema
ghur
Msierah
Gzira
Birkirkara Msida
Gwardamanga Floriana
Hamrun
tormi
Marsamxett Harbour
VALLETTA
Ricasoli Point
Rinella
Kalkara
Il-Wileg
Grand Harbour
Three Cities
Marsa
Paola
Zabbar
Tarxien
Marsaskala
Marsaskala Bay
Luqa
Zejtun
St Thomas Bay
Mqabba
Gudja
Ghaxaq
Mamo Tower
Xrobb il-Ghagin
Kirkop
rendi
Safi
Ghar Dalam
Marsaxlokk
Tas Silg
urrieq
Borg in-Nadur
Birzebbuga
Delimara
gret
Bubaqra
Kalafrana
Marsaxlokk Bay
Delimara Point

which was unique to the islands. Maltese schools have adopted British uniform styles almost exactly, so that in Valletta troops of children neatly dressed in blazers with pocket badges are rather more commonplace than they now are in London. The traffic keeps to the left; policemen wear helmets; pillar-boxes and telephone kiosks are red. Houses have suburban names, often untranslated into Maltese. But the islanders are not the less Maltese because they are proud of being British also. With few exceptions they are Roman Catholic and the trappings of their religion are most typically Mediterranean. Like other Mediterranean peoples they use the street as the extension of their homes. They are devout, hard-working, cheerful, and intelligent.

The *casals*, as the villages are called, though seldom notable for great art, have the charm of an unfamiliar style of architecture with narrow streets designed as much to hinder an enemy as to further friendly progress. Their width served a donkey with panniers for many centuries before the coming of the motor-car. The dgħaisa, the characteristic harbour boat, with a high and painted prow is rowed in traditional fashion standing.

1 VALLETTA AND FLORIANA

A The centre of the city

VALLETTA, or *La Valletta*, the capital of Malta with 17,550 inhab., occupies the seaward half of Mt Sceberras (140 ft), the long rocky promontory which divides Grand Harbour from the harbour of Marsamxett. Founded by Grand Master La Vallette on 28 March 1566 on virgin rock, the city was designed by Franc. Laparelli and completed in 1571 by his assistant Gerolamo Cassar. Its plan comprises a rectangular grid of streets, twelve along and nine across the peninsula, with a perimeter road inside the fortifications. The streets follow the natural terrain with the result that many are steep or rise in steps, Byron's 'cursed streets of stairs'. Segregation of the knights into a Collachium, or inner citadel, was finally abandoned and the Auberges dispersed through the city to sites near the bastion to be defended by each Langue. The plan of the town has been little altered with the years and offers a unique example of a sea-girt fortified city of the Renaissance. Characteristic of the domestic buildings here, as elsewhere in the island, are the ubiquitous enclosed balconies, of painted wood, contrasting gaily with the golden stone. Homely reminders of former British colonial administration emphasize the exuberance (restrained through it is by Sicilian standards) of southern Baroque art.

Arrival by Sea. Landing from cruise ships in Grand Harbour is made at the Custom House, Lascaris Wharf (taxis), whence Liesse Hill leads directly into Valletta, or Crucifix Hill to Floriana. Pedestrians may ascend by lift (1d.) to Upper Barracca Gardens.

Hotels. In *Floriana*: **Phoenicia** (a), 110 R. mostly with bath, outdoor (heated) swimming pool, gardens; **Excelsior** (d), Great Siege Road, opening 1968. In *Valletta*: **Osborne** (b), 50 South St.; **British** (c), 267 St Ursula St., both unpretentious.

Restaurants at the Phoenicia; also in Valletta: *Bologna*, Kingsway/ Archbishop's St.; *Britannia*; *Cordina*.

Post Office, Merchants St.—CABLE AND WIRELESS LTD., St John's Square.

Motor-Buses from KINGSGATE TERMINUS to *Birkirkara* (red); to *Cospicua* and *Vittoriosa* (pea green); to *Rabat* (dark blue); to *Sliema* (Ferry, Savoy, Spinola, etc.; green with dark green band); to *Żabbar* and *Marsaskala* (red with blue band); to *Żebbug* and *Siġġiewi* (yellow with orange band); to *Luqa Airport* and *Żurrieq* (orange). From CASTILE TERMINUS to *Attard* and *Lija* (red with red and white band); to *Tarxien* and *Birzebbuġa* (blue with red and white band); to *Tarxien, Gudja,* and *Għaxaq* (blue with cream band); to *St Paul's Bay, Mellieħa,* also to *Għain Tuffieħa* and *Gozo Ferry* (white with blue band); to *Mosta* and *Naxxar* (brown with dark brown band); to *Żejtun* (red with green band).

Government Tourist Office, Merchants St.—TRAVEL AGENCIES: *Thos Cook & Son*, 20 Kingsway; *American Express*, 14 Zachary St.; *Mifsud Bros.*, 66 South St.

History. A simple watch-tower seems to have stood on the tip of the peninsula when the Knights arrived. To guard the entrance to Grand Harbour Fort St Elmo was built in 1551. The first proposal to fortify Mt Sceberras was made by Strozzi about this time, and Bartolomeo Genga died in Malta in 1559 after being called in as consultant architect. Another plan was drawn up in 1562 by Bald. Lanci of Urbino and the support of Pius IV obtained at the Council of Trent, but nothing had been started when the Turks occupied the peninsula as their base for the Great Siege of Birgu, the Knights' first capital. After the raising of the siege the pope sent Laparelli to La Vallette; within three days of his arrival, he had prepared a new plan for a fortified city and the foundation stone of Valletta was laid on 28 March 1566.

The walled city of Valletta is separated from Floriana, its s.w. extension, by a terreplein, on which is laid out a vast piazza. In the centre plays the grandiose *Triton Fountain* by Vinc. Apap; to either side are the stands of Kingsgate Bus Station. To the w. the Phoenicia Hotel overlooks shady gardens (comp. p. 81). Protecting the city is a dry ditch, 55 ft deep and 30 ft wide, hewn from the solid rock by Turkish slaves, which extends for 950 yds between the two harbours. It is crossed by a bridge, from which (r.) we may see a lower bridge that in 1883–1931 carried a railway from Valletta to Mdina. *Kingsgate*, opening in St James's Curtain and protected by two bastions (see below), was tastelessly rebuilt in 1966. We pass under Queen's Way. The open space to the right, newly arcaded in 1968, is the site of the old railway station (comp. above).

Kingsway, the high street of Valletta, extends N.E. for a mile along the spine of the promontory on which the city is built, terminating at Fort St Elmo. Named originally Strada San Giorgio, it was known during the French occupation as Rue de la République and subsequently as Strada Reale. It is thronged all day, but especially during the evening passeggiata when the traffic is diverted from it. To the right are the melancholy ruins of the *Royal Opera House*, bombed in 1942. Designed by E. M. Barry, it was built (1861–64) on the site allocated to the Auberge of England and had already suffered once by fire in 1873. The *Palazzo della Ferreria*, on the site of the foundry of the Order, opposite, houses the Public Works Department. Beyond, to the right, is *St Barbara*, the church of the Langue of Provence, by Gius. Bonici (1739). The severe façade is adorned with a completely gilded figure of the Virgin. The church now serves English, French, and German catholics. The church of *St Francis*, on the left, rebuilt in 1681, has a celebrated roof painting by Gius. Calì, and is popular for evening devotions.

The **Auberge of Provence,** designed by Gerolamo Cassar in 1571, has a symmetrical façade of two superimposed orders, Doric below, Ionic above. The central portico is given emphasis by the use of paired columns, set forward of the wall in contrast with the engaged pilasters of the wings. Since 1958 the building has housed the **National Museum of Malta,** a collection based on the private accumulation of Grand Master de Rohan, expanded and organized by Sir Themistocles Zammit in 1901–35. Adm. see p. 47.

The entrance hall (with a crude but striking ceiling painting) contains a large relief map of the island showing archaeological sites and a model of Valletta as built by the Knights. On the walls, heraldic fragments from demolished buildings; stele to Giulio Amati, Admiral of the Order, who repaired the quay in 1651. We turn right. NEOLITHIC GALLERY. Wall cases (r. to l.) display chronologically examples of the pottery styles from each phase of Maltese prehistory. *Case* 1. Impressed pottery from Għar Dalam, closely related to the Stentinello ware of Sicily. *Case* 4. Small contemporary stone model of a megalithic building, showing a simple plan and the method of roofing by slabs (c. 2000 B.C.). Later and more complete pottery from the temple sites and from tombs at Xemxija may be related to the models of the temples at Mġarr, Mnajdra, Haġar Qim, and Ġgantija (Gozo), and of the Hypogeum. On the left side of the gallery we may note bead necklaces, the incised Bull and Goat Plate from the Hypogeum, and a series of steatopygous idols from Haġar Qim. In a centre case the famous 'Sleeping Woman', a terracotta figurine from the Hypogeum, representing perhaps a patient or an initiate seeking in sleep an oracular dream (comp. the process of incubation used in Greece at Epidauros and elsewhere).

The TARXIEN ROOM contains further statuettes, including a more realistic skirted figure in terracotta on a straw core (perhaps a priest, rather than a goddess?), more sophisticated pottery, stone hammers and axes, and casts of the crude monumental sculptures from the temple at Tarxien. Tools are displayed of flint, an import from Sicily, and of obsidian, the most likely source of which was the Lipari Islands.

The Bronze Age came to Malta from the E. and the material in the BRONZE AGE ROOM bears no resemblance to and has no continuity with what went before. Objects from the Tarxien cremation cemetery include pottery, axes and daggers in bronze, together with ornaments and carbonized grasses (c. 1450–1350 B.C.). Pottery from the Iron Age village of Baħrija and from Borġ in-Nadur shows that a further wave of migrants arrived from the direction of Sicily and Calabria.

We return to the central lobby and turn right. The small room by the stairs contains various models of temples made in Neolithic times, whether as designer's or mason's working models, objects of piety, or charms is not known; triangular stone anchors; rollers on which the vast slabs were transported. Carved altars and blocks from the temples of Haġar Qim, Buġibba, and Xrobb-il Għaġin. The iron anchors in the corridor outside, raised from the sea bed, are from galleys of the Knights.

The TARXIEN SCULPTURE GALLERY is dominated by the mutilated lower half of a goddess statue originally c. 9 ft high. Opposite is a large block carved with a spiral decoration which may derive from Minoan-Mycenaean patterns. In the corner is a complete *Altar from the first apse of the s. temple group at Tarxien. In the stone cupboard in its face were found a flint knife and the horn of a goat. —Steps mount to the PUNIC AND ROMAN ROOMS, containing well-preserved articles (including Greek imports) from Punic rock tombs. Important are several Phoenician inscriptions, especially a votive cippus from the site of a Temple of Melkart at Tas Silġ (Marsaxlokk) inscribed bilingually in Phoenician and Greek. Terracotta sarcophagus. Contents of tombs of Roman date showing local Punic ware in conjunction with a bowl made at Megara in Greece.

The UPPER FLOOR is devoted to a well-displayed collection of **Paintings,** by *Mattia Preti*, *Matthias Stomer*, *Guido Reni*, and artists of the second rank working in the violent s. Italian style affected by Caravaggio. Sch. of Jan van Scorel, Portrait of a Lady; Roman School, Grand Master Verdala; marble relief plaque of Innocent XI, the expression hardly suggesting the simple and blameless life he undoubtedly led; pleasant water-colours by C. von Bocktorff and G. Schranz, and historical views of Malta of topographical interest. The principal room, with painted ceiling, displays vestments, portraits of Grand Masters, and silver from the hospital of the Santo Spirito. The COIN ROOM is shown on request.

In St John's Square (r.) is the principal entrance to **St John's Co-Cathedral,** built in 1573–77 by G. Cassar, and until 1798 the conventual church of the Order. The entire expense of its erection was defrayed by Grand Master La Cassière and the church was consecrated on 20 Feb 1578. The building, which is remarkable alike for its historical associations, its architectural proportions, the richness of its decoration, and the wonderful diversity of its treasures, was embellished by successive Grand Masters and further enriched by the *gioja*, or present, which every knight was bound by statute to make on promotion. All but a few of the Grand Masters are buried here, their tombs affording a veritable museum of Baroque sculpture. By a decree of Pius VII in 1816 the church was elevated to the status of co-Cathedral with St Peter and St Paul of the old city (p. 102).

In plan the church is a plain rectangle. The severe FAÇADE, flanked by two bell towers, projects on the N. side a little beyond the width of the interior. The portico supports a balcony. The window above was enlarged to provide light for Preti's ceiling (comp. below). In the pediment is a bronze bust of the Saviour by Aless. Algardi; above, a 'Maltese' Cross, of eight points, the symbol of the Knights of Jerusalem. The three faces of the clock, by Clerici, on the s. tower, mark the hour, the day of the month, and the day of the week. Over the door the arms of Pope Gregory XIII are flanked by those of the Order and of La Cassière.

The ***Interior,** ornate but harmonious, consists of a single NAVE, 189 ft long, with side chapels, the separating walls of which buttress the vault. Despite a width of 51 ft, the apex of the slightly pointed tunnel-vault is only 64 ft above the floor. The horizontal line is further emphasized by the lack of entablature. This is replaced by an architrave which continues the pilaster capital mouldings across the intercolumniations. The ritual division of the nave from the choir is marked architecturally by a thickening of the vault rib and its supporting pilasters; as this is extended to the outside buttresses, it may be that a crossing and dome were projected. From Corpus Christi to the Feast of St Peter and St Paul the nave walls are adorned with Flemish *Tapestries*, by Judocus de Vos (1697), based on paintings by Rubens and Poussin. The vault paintings (in oil directly on to primed stonework) were executed by Mattia Preti in 1662–67 at the expense of the Brothers Cotoner. They represent eighteen episodes in the life of St John the Baptist.

The ***Pavement** is composed of some 400 sepulchral slabs laid in memory of the flower of the Order's chivalry. Constituted of marbles of every hue and adorned with coats-of-arms, heraldic emblazonments, military and naval trophies, instruments of music and war, mitres and croziers, figures of angels, crowns and palms of martyrs, skeletons and other symbols of death, the floor produces the gorgeous and striking effect of a stone carpet.

The SANCTUARY, raised on four steps, is closed by a marble balustrade. Within are the thrones of the Queen and of the Archbishop of Malta. The two bronze *Lecterns* were presented by Francis of Lorraine in 1557 to the conventual church of Birgu. The *High Altar* (1686) is of lapis lazuli. Behind is a wooden *Lectern*, beautifully carved with scenes from the life of the Baptist. The gilded 16C *Choir Stalls* return against the E. wall. Above are a pair of organs. There is no E. window; in its stead the apse is filled with a colossal marble group of the Baptism of Christ, by Gius. Mazzuoli.

The **Chapels** were each allotted to a Langue of the Order. The small doors linking them were enlarged and arched by M. Preti to give almost the appearance of aisles. SOUTH SIDE. The CHAPEL OF CASTILE, LEÓN, AND PORTUGAL (*St James*), decorated by Preti, contains the tombs of Manoel Pinto de Fonseca (G.M. 1741–73), and of Manoel de Vilhena (G.M. 1722–36), executed before his death by Massimiliano de Soldanis Benzis; the Grand Master is depicted on the relief panel examining the plan of Fort Manoel. The Byzantine ikon on the altar was brought to Malta in 1760 by the revolted Christian slaves of a Turkish man-of-war.

In the CHAPEL OF ARAGON, Catalonia, and Navarre (*St George*), the altarpiece of St George was painted by Preti in Naples before

1 Vilhena
2 Pinto
3 Nic. Cotoner
4 De Redin
5 Perellos
6 Raf. Cotoner
7 De Chatte–Gessan
8 De Robles y Pereira
9 De Paule
10 Lascaris
11 J. de Wignacourt
12 Adrian de Wignacourt
13 De Rohan–Polduc
14 Louis–Charles d'Orleans
15 Carafa
16 Zondadari

Co-Cathedral of St John

1657 and sent to Malta as a sample of his work. The other paintings, also by Preti, are later. A bronze medallion of Grand Master Ramón Despuig (1736–41) commemorates his decoration of the altar. Two of the four Grand Masters' tombs should be noted: that of Nicolas Cotoner, ascribed to Dom. Guidi, and that of Ramón Perellos (1697–1702), by Gius. Mazzuoli of Volterra. Both artists were admirers of Bernini. The CHAPEL OF AUVERGNE (*St Sebastian*) has two lunettes from the life of the saint, by Gius. d'Arena, though the altarpiece, also attributed to him, more resembles the work of Fil. Paladino. An epitaph in the floor marks the grave of Melchior de Robles y Pereira, who was killed in the siege.

The E. CHAPEL OF THE BLESSED SACRAMENT is closed by a screen and gates of silver (1752). Their colour is said to result from their being painted black in 1798 to escape the French. The Madonna di Carafa, bequeathed by Girol. Carafa, prior of Barletta, in 1617, was moved here in 1954 (Marian Year) from the chapel of Italy. It filled the gap left when the Madonna of Phileremos (originally brought from Rhodes) was removed by Grand Master Hompesch. The 15C crucifix, painted in tempera, also came from Rhodes. The keys on the walls, from Turkish fortresses at Mahometta (Hammamet, between Tunis and Sousse), Lepanto (Navpaktos in Greece), and Passava (near Gytheion in the Peloponnese), were captured by Admiral Gattinara in 1601.

NORTH SIDE. A door in the Sanctuary gives access, through the Chapel of Provence, to the CHAPEL OF THE HOLY RELICS, dedicated to St Charles Borromeo and allotted in 1784–98 to the Anglo-Bavarian Langue. The wooden figure of St John the Baptist on the left wall came from the poop of the Carrack in which the Knights sailed from Rhodes. From the *Chapel of Provence* (St Michael), we descend to the Crypt, which contains the tombs of all the first twelve Maltese Grand Masters save Didier de Saint Jaille. The medieval style of their sarcophagi with full-length effigies is somewhat swamped by Nasini's exuberant decoration. Here, among others, are buried Villiers de l'Isle Adam, hero of the defence of Rhodes (tomb by Antonello Gagini, 1534); Jean Parisot de La Vallette who gave name to the city; Jean l'Eveque de la Cassière, founder of the church; Alof de Wignacourt (of the aqueduct); and the only person here below the rank of grand master, Sir Oliver Starkey, Turkopolier of England and secretary to La Vallette.

The CHAPEL OF FRANCE (*St Paul*) was stripped of its Baroque decoration c. 1840. It contains the tomb of Emmanuel Marie de Rohan-Polduc, last but one of the Grand Masters, who laid the foundation of the Maltese civil code. Also in this chapel are the earliest and latest monuments in the upper church: a simple marble urn of 1615 and the tomb of Louis Charles d'Orléans, count of

Beaujolais, brother of King Louis-Philippe, who died in Malta in
1808; his full-length figure, by Jean-Jacques Pradier, was added in
1844. The CHAPEL OF ITALY (*St Catherine*) has as its altarpiece
Preti's Mystic marriage of St Catherine. To the left of the altar,
St Jerome, painted in Malta by Caravaggio (1608). Beyond the N.
door is the CHAPEL OF GERMANY, dedicated to the Magi. It was
transferred to Germany from England only in 1631 (although the
Langue of England was effectively suppressed by Henry VIII).
The vestibule contains the plain tomb-slab of Mattia Preti (1613–
99), who settled in Malta in 1661 and died here.

The two w. chapels serve as vestibules to transeptal additions to the
church which flank the façade. To the s. is the ORATORY OF ST JOHN,
erected in 1603 to provide a suitable place for knightly devotions and
the instruction of novices, and decorated after 1662 by Preti. It has a
fine 17C organ. Above the altar, Beheading of St John by Caravaggio.
On the altar is the monstrance made by Bernini for the reliquary
containing the right hand of the Baptist; the reliquary was looted by
the French (and went down in the 'Orient' in Aboukir Bay), the relic
was given by Hompesch to Paul I of Russia. Off the N. side are two
sacristies and a treasury (1598). Preti's birth of the Blessed Virgin fills
the lunette over the entrance. Here is displayed a small collection of
pictures, including an altarpiece that once adorned the chapel of the
Langue of England, a 16C triptych of the Deposition, and a portrait
of Preti painted by a pupil. The vestments with the sacred vessels that
escaped Napoleon's sack can be seen only by special arrangement.
Entered from the little cloistral cemetery on the s. side is the *Museum*
(adm. 2/6; weekdays 9–1, 3–5.30), in which the tapestries (see above)
are normally kept.

We may leave St John's by the N. door, which opens into GREAT
SIEGE SQUARE. A portico screens the N. wall of the cathedral. In
the square an allegorical group by Sciortino commemorates the
dead of the Great Siege of 1565. The *Law Courts*, opposite, replaced in 1967 the Auberge of Auvergne (an austere edifice of 1574
ruined by a bomb in 1942). A cinema in St Lucia's St. (l.) occupies
the site of the house where Garibaldi stayed in 1864 (plaque).

Farther on we reach QUEEN'S SQUARE. To the left the Casino
Maltese, the principal social club of the island, occupies the former
Treasury of the Order. A marble statue of Queen Victoria (1897),
by Giuseppe Valenti, stands before the arcaded façade of the **Royal
Malta Library**, or *Biblioteca*, designed in 1786 by Stef. Ittar, a
Calabrian architect, for the Order and completed in 1796. The
collections now include 61,000 books, 50 incunabula, and 1250
MSS., as well as the records of the Università (or commune) from
1350 to 1818, and the priceless archives of the Order (6524 vols.
of MSS.). The hours of admission vary slightly day by day, but
the library is always open, Mon–Sat, 8.30–1.

In 1555 the Knights established a library where the books of their
deceased brethren could be deposited, and passed a statute in 1612 forbidding the sale of a Knight's books at his death. The great bequests of
Card. Giocchino (5670 vols) in 1760 and of Guerin de Tencin (9700

vols) in 1763 necessitated provision of a new building, which was decreed in 1776 and paid for by Perez de Sarrio. At the same time it was decided that the library should be opened to the public. The transfer of books may have been delayed by the French invasion for the building seems not to have been inaugurated until 1812.

The entrance steps are adorned with a bust of Dun Karm, composer of the Hymn of Malta. A selection from the archives is permanently displayed. They include (despite some losses during the French occupation) documents from c. 1083 to 1798: deed of Baldwin I of Jerusalem (1107) giving land, the bull of Paschal II instituting the Order (1113), some of the records of the Templars before their suppression in 1312, letters from most European monarchs, the act of Donation of 1530 by the Emp. Charles V, minutes of councils from 1459, bulls of the chancellery from 1346, and the proofs of nobility submitted for admittance to the Order. A beautiful exhibit is the illuminated life of St Anthony the Abbot, by Master Robin Fournier of Avignon (1426).

Old Theatre St. descends (l.) to the Anglican cathedral (p. 000); between the library and the Palace (r.) is a busy street market, popularly known as 'Fuq il-Monti'.

Beyond extends PALACE SQUARE, where Dun Mikiel Xerri and 33 companions were shot by the French in 1798 for planning to open the city gates to the besieging islanders. The Palace fronts directly on to the street and the attention is drawn first to the *Main Guard* which faces it. This once accommodated the Grand Master's bodyguard and the Chancery of the Order. An inscription on the portico records the cession of Malta to Great Britain. Later the building was occupied by the Garrison Library and the palace quarterguard, which had its mess above. The staircase preserves a painting of an unfortunate captain of the guard who tripped over his sword on the descent. The building, which now houses the Commonwealth and Foreign Affairs Office, is admirably set off by the flamboyant Hostel de Verdelin on the corner of Archbishop's Street.

The **Palace of the Grand Masters,** begun in 1571 by Gerolamo Cassar for Grand Master del Monte, incorporates the house erected for the master's nephew Eustachio two years earlier. This forms the N.W. corner of the palace and its balconies were matched for the sake of symmetry at the far end. The façade is 266 ft long and given coherence mainly by the roof line, unified in the late 17C, and by the balancing Baroque gateways which, in the time of G. M. Pinto (1741–73), replaced a single archway. The palace remained the official residence of the grand masters until 1798 and continued as that of successive governors and of the governor-general. It is also the seat of the House of Representatives.

The right-hand gateway (or the entrance from Queen's Square) gives access to PRINCE ALFRED'S COURT, with a stately Norfolk

Island pine. The clock, placed here by Pinto in 1745, has figures in Turkish costume to strike the hours. Below is the entrance to the *Armoury (adm. see p. 47). A modern staircase mounts to the great hall of the Knights, 253 ft by 38, which runs the full length of the palace above Merchants St. By a statute of 1551 all arms and armour belonging to the Knights were pooled and kept in order at the public expense. The collection, though deficient in early armour and reduced by later neglect from c. 25,000 suits to under 6000 pieces, ranks in interest if not in richness, within the confines of its period, with those of the Armeria Real in Madrid and the Tower of London. It narrowly escaped removal to the Tower in 1827 and to Woolwich in 1846. Among many soldiers' suits are more resplendent ceremonial examples made for La Vallette and Wignacourt (Milanese, inlaid with gold); sapping armour of Wignacourt, of immense weight; fragments supposedly worn by Dragut during the siege; captured Turkish shields. Souvenirs of the second siege include the George Cross with the citation in the hand of George VI, and the now fragmentary remnant of 'Faith', sole survivor of the three Gladiator fighters put up by the R.A.F. to defend the island.

From King Alfred's Court steps descend to PRINCE OF WALES'S COURT, entered also from Kingsway by the left-hand gate. Here amid hibiscus and palm-trees stands a bronze *Statue of Neptune*, originally placed by Alof de Wignacourt as the centrepiece of a fountain in the old fishmarket in 1615; it has been conjectured to derive from a work by Giambologna, and to represent Andrea Doria. Behind under the arcade is a marble fountain with an elaborately carved escutcheon of Ramon Perellos. From the court a circular staircase, having shallow steps and wide enough to accommodate the grand master's litter, ascends to the STATE APARTMENTS (which may be viewed when not in use; apply to officials at head of stairs).

To the right the long *Armoury Corridor*, lined with portraits and armour, leads between the two courts; ahead extends the *Entrance Corridor*, similarly adorned with with a canvas ceiling painted by Nic. Nasini da Siena. In the lunettes above the windows are depicted naval battles of the Order. The three doors on the left of the Entrance Corridor lead into the *Hall of St Michael and St George*, formerly the Supreme Council chamber of the Knights. The frieze is painted with twelve incidents of the Great Siege, executed by Matteo da Lecce, a pupil of Michelangelo better known from his work in Seville as Mateo Pérez de Alisio. The hall acquired its present name in 1818 when the first investiture of the newly created British order was held here. At one end the throne used by the Governor-General stands on a dais; opposite is a sculptured wooden gallery with six cinquecento panels depicting scenes from Genesis. This was formerly in the palace chapel and may derive

Valletta

0	100	200	300	Yards
0	100	200	300	Metres

ARBOUR

S Sebastian Curtain

Serge Aragon

Curia

Auberge of Bavaria

English Curtain

St Gregory's Bastion

St Gregory's Curtain

Ball's Bastion

French Curtain

Fort St Elmo

FOUNTAIN STREET

STREET

T R E E T

R E E T

K I N G S W A Y

Palace

ST ELMO PLACE

Abercrombie's Bastion

Greek th.Church

STORE ET

Breakwater

University

Hospital of the Knights (ruined)

Abercrombie's Curtain

CHRISTOPHER STREET

ST DOMINIC STREET

HOSPITAL STREET

NORTH ST.

STREET

St Lazarus Bastion

STREET

St Lazarus Curtain

IRISH

Lower Barracca

Curtain

Fish Market

ARBOUR

from a galley of the Order. The door to the left of the dais admi
to the Red State Room, or *Hall of the Ambassadors*, the Gran
Master's audience chamber. Below the coffered ceiling runs
frieze of scenes from the history of the Order between 1309 an
1524. The portraits include *Vanloo*, Louis XV; *Levitzky*, Catheri
II of Russia; and *Lionello Spada*, Alof de Wignacourt, wearir
the armour noted above (the painting was badly restored in 1886
The Yellow State Room, formerly the *Paggeria*, is the first roo
opening from the Prince of Wales Corridor. It contains a canva
of Jacob as a shepherd, by *Ribera*. The remaining rooms in th
wing are occupied by the Governor-General and his staff (no adm.

Off the Armoury Corridor is the Council Chamber of the Orde
known as the *Tapestry Chamber* from the set of Gobelins tapestri
presented by Perellos and signed by Le Blondel. Here now del
berate the **House of Representatives**.

The House consists of 50 members, elected on a system of pr
portional representation. The Parliament of Malta consists of H.M
the Queen and the House of Representatives; the executive authority
the Queen is exercised on her behalf by the Governor-General.

Beyond the staircase and overlooking Palace Square is the *Sta
Dining Room.*—Coleridge occupied 'a suite of delightfully cosy ar
commanding rooms' during his residence in 1804–5 first as priva
Secretary to Sir Alexander Ball and later as Secretary to the Gover
ment of Malta. Some thirty years earlier Cagliostro was for a tin
G. M. Pinto's resident magician.

Kingsway beyond Palace Square becomes less interesting as it de
cends to Fort St Elmo (Rte 1c). The only important building is th
Borsa (Exchange).

Archbishop's St. descends parallel to Old Theatre St. (com
above) to Independence Square, crossing three of the streets th
run parallel with Kingsway.

The first, STRAIT STREET (Strada Stretta), had a notorious reputatic
even in the days of the Knights, who disguised their duels there
casual quarrels occasioned by a collision in the narrow thoroughfar
since premeditated duelling was severely punished. In both Wor
Wars it was known to servicemen as 'The Gut' and its more di
reputable bars catered freely for a variety of tastes.

On the corner of Old Bakery St. is a much buttressed old buildi
that formerly housed a school, and beyond Old Mint St. (r.) is th
Curia, or Archbishop's Palace, well restored in 1953. Facing Ind
pendence Square is the *Auberge of Aragon*, one of the plainest of th
knightly headquarters, by Cassar; it is now the official residen
of the Prime Minister. **St Paul's Anglican Cathedral** occupies th
site of the Auberge of Germany, which was demolished in 1838
make way for it. The church, to a design by Richard Lankershee
was built by William Scamp at the expense of the dowager Que
Adelaide, widow of William IV, in 1839–41. Its prominent Goth
spire combines not unpleasingly with the classical style of the ma
edifice, their juxtaposition at ground level being hidden from vie

y clever siting. The organ was formerly in Chester cathedral. A
laque on St Paul's Buildings, beyond the apse, records Sir Walter
cott's brief stay at the Beverley Hotel on this site in 1831.

Unobtrusive in Old Theatre St. is the **Manoel Theatre**, built in
731 and claimed to be the oldest theatre in the Commonwealth,
hough 150 years junior in Europe to Vicenza's Teatro Olimpico.
The interior was beautifully restored in 1960. Admission (from
Old Mint St.) 10–12, also 3–4.40 in winter; 1/-. The church of the
Carmine, opposite, is being rebuilt (1968). At No. 52 Old Bakery
St. Dun Karm (comp. above) lived in 1910–36. The Bakery of the
Order used to occupy the block, farther w., between St John's St.
and Britannia St.

Returning to Palace Square and taking Archbishop's St. in the
opposite direction, we pass the Greek Catholic Church and come
o Merchants St., after Kingsway the most important thoroughfare
n Valletta. The ROYAL UNIVERSITY OF MALTA began as a Jesuit
college, instituted in 1592 by Pope Clement VIII, with faculties
of philosophy and theology. In 1769, after the expulsion of the
Jesuits from the island, Grand Master Emmanuel Pinto raised the
college to university status, incorporating in it as a faculty of
medicine the School of Anatomy founded by Nicholas Cotoner in
1674. The Royal patronage was granted by George VI in 1937.
There are now six faculties. The Jesuit buildings are substantially
unaltered and the church of Gesù is now the university church. If it
was built in 1592–1600, it cannot have been designed (as is usually
stated) by either of the Bonamici (Filippo or Francesco) since
neither was yet born. In the left transept an inscription records the
consecration here of Fabio Chigi (later Pope Alexander VII) as
Inquisitor of the Order.

Above the high altar, Circumcision, attr. to *Bald. Peruzzi;* chapel of
St Ignatius (r.), altarpiece by *Romanelli;* 3rd chapel (l.), *G.B. Caracciolo*,
Flight into Egypt; 2nd chapel (l.), *Mattia Preti*, Altarpiece and two
lunettes.

We pass between the rear façade of the Magisterial Palace and
the animated covered *Market*, built in iron in 1859–62, where
exotic fish and fruits provide a colourful display. Beyond Fuq
il-Monti (comp. above), the former *Banca Giuratale*, or Town Hall,
an elegant building of c. 1720, is now the Public Registry. Opposite
is the *Monte di Pietà*, a government pawnbroking department,
established on the continental model in the 16C and moved here
by G. M. Ximenes. Behind this, in St Paul's St., the church of *St
Paul Shipwrecked*, with an altarpiece of the shipwreck by Fil.
Paladino.

On the next corner a plaque marks the site of the house of Sir
Oliver Starkey. The main offices of Barclay's Bank overlook the
cloistered graveyard of the co-cathedral. At the corner of St
John's St. is a column believed to have been a pillory or whipping-

post. Beyond (l.), the Department of Public Health occupies th
Castellania of the Order, begun in 1748 by Gius. Bonici. Here th
Castellano presided over the court of civil and criminal law. Th
pleasantly balanced façade has a centrepiece by Maestro Gian witl
figures of Justice and Truth.

The sober *Palazzo Parisio*, where Gen. Bonaparte lodged for
week in June 1798 on his way to Egypt, now houses the Genera
Post Office. From the street in front the post-bus departs for Gozo
Opposite is the *Auberge of Italy*. The building, begun by Gerol
Cassar in 1574, was improved and enlarged (probably by the ad
dition of the top story) by Grand Master Carafa who, in 1683
placed his effigy and inscription above the rusticated portal. Onc
the headquarters of the Royal Engineers, it later housed the mu
seum, and in 1968 the Law Courts, which are soon to be moved t
their new building in Kingsway. Adjacent, but with its façade o
Victory Square, is the church of the Langue of Italy, *St Catherine's*
designed by Gerol. Cassar in 1576, with a porch added in 1713
The interior, octagonal in plan, has an altarpiece of the Martyrdon
of St Catherine by Mattia Preti; notable also, Our Lady of Sorrows
by Benedetto Luti.

Facing is *Our Lady of Victory*, or La Vittoria, the first building to b
erected in Valletta in thanksgiving for the Turkish defeat. The façad
was added before 1690 when Ramon Perellos placed a bust of Innocen
XI above the central window. Outside the church annually (Sun. afte
16 Jan) pet animals are blessed.

We turn left into Castile Place (bus station) passing in front of th
*Auberge of Castile, the grandest and most harmonious example c
Maltese Baroque, reconstructed by Cachia for G. M. Pinto in 174
and probably inspired by the Prefettura at Lecce. The portal i
flanked by massive bronze cannons; above, the arms of Emmanue
Pinto are conspicuously displayed. The building now serves a
military headquarters. Castile Place is bounded by the massive wal
of *St James's Cavalier*, which now shelters the shop of the Navy
Army, and Air Force Institutes. From the E. corner of the square
to the left of the Garrison Church, open **Upper Barracca Gardens**
with a terrace affording a magnificent vantage-point over Gran
Harbour. Originally an exercise-ground of the Langue of Italy
the space was given roofed arcades in 1661 but the roofs were re
moved in 1771 after a conspiracy had been hatched within thei
shelter. Among the statues in the gardens 'Les Gavroches', afte
the inspiration of Hugo's gamins, is considered the masterpiec
of Sciortino, and there are monuments to Lord Strickland and t
various heroes of the past. Below is the saluting battery.

In the corner a huge passenger lift descends to Lascaris Whar
(Rte 1 c).

Between St James's Cavalier and the Vernon Club, Queensway
crosses Kingsgate to St John's Cavalier, on the bastion of whicl

are laid out the *Hastings Gardens*. The gardens, which contain a monument to the Marquess of Hastings, governor in 1824–27, are continued along the curtain to St Michael's Bastion and afford good views towards Mosta and Mdina.

B. Floriana

FLORIANA, a suburban extension of Valletta, was laid out to a plan of 1724 within the forward line of defences erected in the grand-mastership of de Paule and takes name from their architect.

In 1634 in face of a threatened new Turkish attack, Urban VIII sent Paolo Floriana to Grand Master de Paule to advise on additional defences. The Floriana lines were started in 1636, held up when the Margherita lines (Rte 4) were begun in 1638, but resumed in 1640 after a visit by Giovanni de' Medici. They were eventually completed by Grunenberg and de Tigné. The existing street plan dates from 1724–28 and many of the central blocks from before 1760.

Leaving Valletta by Castile Place we descend Duke of York Avenue. Below on the left *Kalkara Gardens* occupy a terrace above the now deserted building of the King George V Hospital and afford a fine view of Senglea and its creeks across Grand Harbour. To our right a deep ditch protects *St James' Counter-guard*. At the bottom of the hill stands the *War Memorial*. Behind it (l.) the local headquarters of NATO conspicuously flies the flags of treaty powers. Pleasant gardens extend N. to the Phoenicia Hotel (comp. Rte 1A). Prominent in their centre a golden eagle crowns the *R.A.F. Memorial* and in front of the hotel a *Monument to Christ the King*, by Ant. Sciortino, commemorates the International Eucharistic Conference of 1913.

To the w. extend THE MALL and the parallel Sarria St. Between them the *Maglio Gardens*, a tree-lined walk, was originally laid out by Grand-Master Lascaris as a ground for young knights to exercise at Pall-mall, in order to divert their thoughts from women, wine, and gambling. A statue of Vilhena that once adorned Fort Manoel, stands at the entrance and the monuments to various Maltese worthies include one to Sir Adrian Dingli unveiled by Edward VII during his second visit to Malta as king in 1907. On the right a huge *Parade Ground* is now used principally for cricket and football by local schools. ST PUBLIUS SQUARE (l.), patterned by the circular slabs that cover its subterranean granaries, admirably sets off the façade of *St Publius*, the huge parish church of Floriana, erected in 1733–68. The design is attributed to Gius. Bonici. The side chapels and their external screen walls were added in 1856. Beyond is the little church of *Sarria*, built on a circular plan by Lorenzo Gafà in 1678. It is adorned with seven vigorous paintings by Preti. Opposite, at the end of the Mall, is a circular water-tower of the Wignacourt aqueduct (comp. Rte 9). The two are set off by the incongruous but not unpleasing Gothic of the Methodist church. On a bastion (r.) the *Argotti Gardens*, administered by the university, contain a fine collection of cacti, exotic trees, and flora of the islands.

From the end of the Mall, St Chalcedonius St. leads past Police Headquarters and through the defences by Notre Dame Gate. By a steep descent under Salvatore Bastion, Sa Maison Rd., its continuation, passes below *Sa Maison Garden* (reopened in 1968; view) and through the outer defences to reach Pietà Creek (Rte 2).

We descend to join ST ANNE ST., the broad arcaded main street of Floriana. The road out passes the *Porte des Bombes*, a cere- monial gate erected in 1697–1720 and now isolated from the walls. Turning back we see in a garden (r.) a striking bronze of Dante. We may return by *Gunlayer Square*, where gardens laid out along the bastions command the docks and anchorages of Grand Harbour.

C. The Fortifications

The Fortifications of Valletta, to the design of Laparelli, were erected between 1566 and 1570 and are structurally largely un- altered. Where they are not still occupied by military establishments, they are in some measure derelict, with the result that it is not usually possible to penetrate within the cavaliers and ravelins. Some of the walks and gardens on the bastions and along the curtains have been described above, but the best idea of the magnitude of the constructions is obtained by walking their circuit. The walk (c. 1½ hrs), affords in addition the varied panoramas of the two harbours and a convenient way of visiting Valletta's peripheral monuments.

From the Vilhena statue in the Mall, GREAT SIEGE ROAD des- cends between the Phoenicia Hotel and Lintorn Barracks under the defences of Valletta. To the right rise the protecting walls sur- rounding St John's Bastion (p. 54) and St Michael's Counter- guard. The entrance to a laundry (r.) admits to part of the outer ditch (from which by a long flight of steps it is possible to regain Kingsgate Bus Station). On our left and below, the Excelsior Hotel (opening in 1968) will occupy St Roque's cove and command excellent views of Marsamxett Harbour. We reach the rocky shore and turn E. some 45 ft above the water.

On the right a road (restricted access) leads through the man-made canyon that constitutes the Great Ditch to Grand Harbour. Passing inland between St Michael's Counterguard and St Michael's Bastion, it serves service establishments amid the rock-cut defences. It passes under Kingsgate bridge and Duke of York Avenue and beyond the Barracca lift joins Lascaris Wharf.—To the left there is a splendid view of Manoel Island (comp. Rte 2) with Ta' Xbiex farther left and Dragut Pt out to the right.

Great Siege Road now rounds *St Andrew's Bastion*, beyond which we curve over the lower Marsamxett Coast Road (with a popular bathing place) to pass within the curtain wall. Marsamxett St. fronts Delmonte Square which, with the two populous streets behind, is set at an angle to the grid plan of Valletta. Here a natural cleft was partly worked to form a '*Manderaggio*' (comp. the Mandraki of Rhodes), or sheltered harbour. For a time builders of houses had to take stone from this site, but the project was abandoned unfinished.

From Delmonte Square St John's St. mounts to the Cathedral.

Beyond *San Salvatore Bastion*, a popular belvedere, we pass below the conspicuous spire of the Anglican cathedral along the *German Curtain*. We turn the corner of St Sebastian St. and pass in front of the Carner Palace (1696), in which the Anglo-Bavarian Langue was installed during its short existence in 1783–98, and which is now a school. The auberge stands above the inconspicuous *Jews' Sally Port*, which readmits to the city from Marsamxett Coast Road (comp. above). The *English Curtain* continues to an ancient sentry-box on the next corner whence the *French Curtain* extends to Fort St Elmo.

Fort St Elmo, the headquarters of the Malta Land Force (no adm.) occupies the whole of the point commanding the entrances to both harbours.

Fort St Elmo had its origin in a watch tower which is first mentioned in 1481 and took name from a small chapel dedicated to the patron saint of fishermen. A fort was erected in 1488 and strengthened in 1551 by Prior Strozzi. The main work was star-shaped with a protecting ravelin facing Marsamxett harbour and a cavalier on the sea front communicating with the main work by a wooden bridge. This was the fortress that in 1565 defied the whole might of the Turkish army for 31 days.

The Turks encamped on Mt Sceberras, placing their batteries on the Marsamxett flank where they were screened from the fire of St Angelo. This left open communication between Birgu and St Elmo of which the Knights at first made full use. Fourteen guns operating from a range of 180 yds kept up a continuous barrage. A sortie to destroy the battery was countered by a janissary attack which stormed the counter scarp. On 3 June the Turks captured the ravelin by surprise and but for a Spanish officer who held the drawbridge single-handed would have captured the fort itself. Here the Turks mounted two guns, soon reducing the ramparts of the fort to rubble. Dragut now constructed a battery on the point that still bears his name. Further assaults were repulsed. Dragut placed another battery on Ricasoli Pt and extended the lines in front of St Elmo to the water in order to cut the garrison's communication with Birgu. While directing these works. Dragut was mortally wounded. An assault on 22 June was again beaten off, a relief attempt from St Angelo was frustrated by the batteries, and on 23 June St Elmo fell. The operation had cost the Turks 8000 men.

Under Alof de Wignacourt the Vendome bastion was added, and in 1687 Grunenberg enclosed the entire point with a bastioned line, to which Grand Master Perellos added further works, so that it is difficult now to imagine the circumstances of the Great Siege. During the rebellion of the priests against G. M. Ximenes, the conspirators captured the fortress. The casemates that now serve as barracks were designed by Tigné in 1790. Captain Ball, first governor of the island, is buried in one bastion and Sir Ralph Abercromby in another. Both bastions and the Cavalier were again reconstructed to modern needs in 1871–75.

The road zigzags in front of the main entrance to St Elmo where more subterranean *Granaries* of the Order are marked by the familiar circular covering slabs. *St Lazarus Bastion* is built over, but its curtain, fronting the hospital, commands a good view of the entrance to Grand Harbour and the *St Elmo Breakwater* built in 1861 to protect it from N.E. gales and its warships from torpedo attack. The iron bridges that once spanned the small boat passage, just under the fort, were brought down by explosive motor-boats in a brave but abortive Italian attack on Grand Harbour on the night of 25 July 1941.

The **Great Hospital of the Order,** or *Sacra Infirmeria*, is sadly only a shell after the bombing and shows an unbroken façade to the harbour only by virtue of minimal restoration. The hospital, built before 1575 by an unknown architect, is externally singularly unimpressive, which may account for its recent neglect. Its plan seems to have been inspired by the Santo Spirito in Rome and the great ward, one of the longest rooms in Europe (503 ft), was well appointed if badly lit. In winter it was hung with 131 pieces of woollen tapestry; in summer adorned with 85 paintings by Mattia Preti. The second great court fronting on Merchants St. was added in the second half of the 17C.

The hospital was placed on the s.e. seafront of the town so 'that patients might be landed from ships at the mouth of the harbour, and brought in by a covered way below the sea wall into the lower ward, without making a tedious and dangerous circuit of the streets'. Its comparatively unhealthy site, sheltered from more bracing winds but open to the enervating sirocco, did not prevent it becoming the most famous institution of its kind in Europe. The patients, who were admitted from outside the Order, ate from silver plate, and the hospital also cared for the insane and for destitute and illegitimate children. The French ejected its patients (and melted down the plate to pay for the Egyptian campaign), but it was reopened by the British as a military hospital and survived until 1919 when it became the headquarters of the Malta police.

Lower Barracca Gardens, occupying part of Castile Bastion above Mġerbeb Point, with a view across the entrance of Grand Harbour towards the Bighi Hospital, have an absurdly charming memorial to Sir Alexander Ball in the form of a Doric temple. *Castille Curtain* and *St Barbara Bastion* continue to a point in the walls below the Franciscan convent and church of *Ta Ġesù*, where a natural cleft has resulted in an area of complex levels and steps. Here the *Victoria Gate* gives access by Liesse Hill to the **Marina.** The church of *Notre-Dame de Liesse*, on the descent, was rebuilt in 1740 at the expense of the Langue of France and is a graceful composition on a circular plan. Best seen from the walls above is the fine low dome moulded with bands of curved stone.

In the time of the Knights the former narrow Del Monte Gate and Nixmangiari Steps served as access to the city. The new gate and road were constructed in 1884–87 and gave vehicular access to travellers arriving by sea. Since air transport became the norm this approach is seldom used except by cruise passengers, and regular bus services have all but killed the ferry approach from the Three Cities.

The name of *Barriera Wharf*, where the fish market now stands, dates from before 1643 when it was used as a place of quarantine. Grand Master Lascaris turned the foreshore into a commercial wharf, building warehouses on both sides of the *Tunnel* by which he pierced the bastion bearing his name. On Lascaris Wharf stands the *Custom House, the graceful masterpiece of Gius. Bonici (1774). Almost opposite is the Barracca Lift. To the s.w. Crucifix Hill ascends to Floriana.

PINTO WHARF continues along the shore below Floriana's defences to the main passenger ship berths. All along are warehouses inaugurated by various grand masters from Cotoner to Pinto.—From the top of Liesse Hill steps at the end of Battery St. ascend to the entrance of the Upper Barracca.

2 SLIEMA AND ST JULIAN'S

ROAD, c. 6 m.; to Sliema c. 3½ m. BUSES (dark green) from Kingsgate to *Ferry*, every few min.; to *Spinola* every 10 min. Though the traffic is not light, this is still a not unpleasant coastal walk.

At the landward end of Floriana, beyond the Porte des Bombes, we diverge right (vehicles left, passing beneath the Hamrun road) and descend Princess Melita Road. On the left is the Protestant cemetery of Ta Braxia; on the right Jubilee Grove, a fine plantation, hides the glacis of Floriana's outer defences. At the foot of the hill, by a small children's park opened by Prince Philip in 1960, Sa Maison Road (p. 70) winds off into the defences. Marina St. follows the shore of Pietà and Msida Creeks, skirting Gwarda-manġa Hill on the top of which, in the district called **Pietà** (*Sa Maison Hotel*, opp. Prince Philip Park) rises the unlovely bulk of St Luke's Hospital and medical school.

The Villa Gwardamanġa is said to have been the residence of the Grand Master's taster. Occupied by Earl Mountbatten, it gave hospitality to Princess Elizabeth while the Duke of Edinburgh was on Malta station.

At the head of MSIDA CREEK the road divides at a roundabout. Msida and Birkirkara lie ahead (comp. Rte 10B); the direct road to Sliema via Gzira branches right. Though longer it is more pleasant to keep to the shore of Msida Creek, past *St Joseph's*, the parish church of Msida, and take the less frequented road via

Sliema

0   500   Yards
0   500 Metres

an's Point
Julian's Tower

TOWER   ROAD

j   i

Sliema Point

☐ Tower

Għar id-Dud

HIGH STREET

SLIEMA

f

STELLA MARIS STREET

h

SLIEMA STREET

HIGH STREET

Stella
Maris
Church   Cinema

QUISISANA

TOWER

PLACE

e

ST RUDOLPH STREET

g

ROAD

k

Cinema

Cambridge
Battery

Cinema

Ferry

TIGNE SEA FRONT

l

ROAD

PRINCE OF WALES ROAD

THE STRAND

P.O.

× Holy Trinity

Sliema Creek

MANOEL ISLAND

Fort Manoel

Lazzaretto

Yacht Harbour

Lazzaretto Creek

Ta'Xbiex. All along the creek yacht berths were under construction in 1968. Across the water the hotels of Floriana are prominent as we round another point into LAZZARETTO CREEK, once (as its name implies) the quarantine anchorage. It is now the principal *Yacht Basin* and always lined with sea-going pleasure crusiers. At the head of the creek, by pleasant gardens, we join an alternative road from Msida (comp. above). We are now in **Gzira**, which has developed largely since 1965 as a residential area with light motor industries.

A bridge on the right leads to **Manoel Island**, where FORT MANOEL, built by de Tigné and de Mondion in 1723–32 for Grand Master Manoel de Vilhena, was designed for a garrison of 500 men. Here in 1800 the French garrison was interned until (after the Treaty of Amiens) the men were returned to France in British ships. The island, previously called Bishop I., was first used as a quarantine station by the Knights, who erected an infectious disease hospital, the *Lazaretto of San Rocco*, before 1643. Though in ruins or in popular occupation, a great part of the lazaretto still stands, its graceful arcaded frontage on the sea forming a familiar landmark from the ramparts of Valletta.

Bad outbreaks of plague occurred in 1592–93, 1623, 1655, and 1675–76, and earlier quarantine stations had been set up on Corradino Heights and below the Del Monte Gate in Valletta. When Grand Master Lascaris appropriated the Barriera to commercial use (comp. Rte 1c), he moved the quarantine station to Bishop I. Cotoner altered the buildings in 1670; Carafa initiated new works in 1683; and Vilhena made improvements when he built the fort. By the mid-18C a disinfection station to accommodate 1000 transients had evolved, which dealt with crews, passengers, cargoes, and mail from all ships with foul bills of health arriving from the Levant. Ships with clean bills merely lay off Sa Maison for 18 days; the period of 'great quarantine' against bubonic plague was 80 days. The laws regarding avoidance of quarantine were strict, involving penalty of death. Mail was disinfected by cutting vertical slits and immersing letters in vinegar, then fumigated by sulphur or saltpetre. The system seems to have been effective, for the only major outbreak in later years occurred in 1813. Plague disappeared from Europe in 1841 and from the Near East soon afterwards, and modern prophylactic methods superseded strict quarantine. The lazaretto continued in use as an isolation hospital and during the First World War admitted wounded from the Dardanelles and sick from the Salonika campaigns. In 1922 it became a clearing house for refugees from Smyrna. During an outbreak of plague in Tunis in 1929 incoming mail was again fumigated in Malta, and the lazaretto was last used during an epidemic in 1936. Evacuated by the Health Department in 1940, the buildings served until 1949 as the base of a submarine flotilla. Opinion about their future is divided between restoration as a historic monument and demolition to make way for a yachting centre. (The medieval word 'lazaretto' is now spelled Lazzaretto when applied to the creek.)

Beyond Manoel Island we skirt *Sliema Creek*, once a busy anchorage of the Royal Navy.

SLIEMA, the second biggest town in Malta (24,000 inhab.), occupies the large irregular peninsula that encloses Marsamxett Harbour on the N.W. On its S. shore the Strand runs along the sea wall of Sliema Creek, whereas, on the N., Tower Road faces the open sea above an extended rocky shore favoured for bathing. The Tigné peninsula runs S.E. from the larger one to end in Dragut Point.

Hotels. *In Sliema:* **Tigne Court** (e), Qui-si-Sana, with swimming pool; **Astra** (f), 127 Tower Road; **Imperial** (g), 1 Rudolph St., with swimming pool; **Capua Court** (h), 60 Victoria Avenue; **Meadowbank** (i), **Crown** (j), 164 and 166 Tower Road; **Plevna** (k), Thornton St.; with swimming pool; **Fortina** (l), Tigne Sea Front; **Preluna, Promenade,** both Tower Road; **Eden Rock,** 117 Tower Road; **New Metropole,** 50 Dingli St., and others. *In St Julian's:* **Sheraton** (a), **Hilton** (b), **Cavalieri,** Spinola Road, all opened 1967; **The Palms** (c); **Villa Rosa** (d), St George's Bay, all these with swimming pools.

Restaurant. *City Gem* (dinner only), St Pius V St. (The Strand).

Post Office, Prince of Wales Road. ENGLISH CHURCH, *Holy Trinity,* Rudolph St.

Amusements. CINEMAS in The Strand and Tower Road opposite Ferry bus station. SWIMMING at Villa Rosa Beach Club. WATER SKIING, sailing, etc. in St Julian's Bay. CASINO at Dragonara Palace.

The centre of Sliema may be placed where the Strand broadens between its junction with Prince of Wales Road and St Anne Square. Here is 'FERRY' bus terminus (though a regular ferry to Valletta no longer plies) and the landing stage (tour of the harbour twice daily at 10.30 and 3.30; 15/-). TOWER ROAD, where at No. 9 Edward Lear stayed in 1865–66, crosses the base of the Tigné Peninsula, the greater part of which is inaccessible; within the military bounds is *Fort Tigné,* built at the order of Emmanuel de Rohan by the Chevalier Tigné in 1792 on the site of the siege headquarters of Dragut.

The principal attraction of Sliema is the coastal drive or walk from Għar-id-Dud Square, where Tower Road meets Quisisana Place, to St Julian's and St George's Bay. Beyond *St Julian's Tower,* one of De Redin's defensive outposts, a fashionable promenade affords pleasant views across St Julian's Bay. Main St., **St Julian's,** turns an abrupt corner to round BALLUTA BAY. Here we meet the farther end of Prince of Wales Road (named for its inaugurator in 1862), which crosses the peninsula as two long hills. At SPINOLA BAY, with a fishing community, is the Spinola terminus of the Sliema buses. Hence the road crosses inland of *Paceville,* a district where the erection of the Hilton Hotel on the site of the former Fort Spinola presages the development of a hitherto neglected stretch of coast. At the top of the hill, beyond the walled garden of the Spinola Palace (1688), St Andrew's Road bears left for St Paul's Bay (Rte 10A), while we continue by St George's Road past the Cable and Wireless Offices. To the right a by-road leads to the *Dragunara Palace,* a sumptuous classical villa now transformed into a casino. Adm 2/- (Sat 5/-) from 8 p.m. (7 on Sun and holidays) for roulette, baccarat, black-jack, etc.; restaurant. Our road ends at **St George's Bay,** commanded on the far side by St George's Barracks, built of local stone with graceful arcades and balustrades. These form part of Pembroke camp (comp. Rte 10A).

3 TOUR OF THE HARBOURS

STEAMER from 'Ferry' Sliema (comp. Rte 2), twice daily. The tour of the harbours (2 hrs.) should on no account be missed. The main interest is now in the seaward view of the historical defences, the busy kaleidoscope of maritime activity that used to characterize the many creeks being now largely a nostalgic memory. The occasional visits of foreign navies and summer calls by cruise ships can greatly heighten the atmosphere. A commentary is provided during the voyage and only an identification of the principal points of interest is given below in the order of normal sailing. Most of the buildings are described in detail in Rtes 1, 2 and 4.

The steamer turns s. across *Sliema Creek* towards MANOEL ISLAND, headquarters of a submarine flotilla in the Second World War. The star-shaped angle towers of *Fort Manoel* rise behind the rocky shore. Farther round the water laps the graceful arcades of the deserted *Lazaretto*. Yachts now line both shores of the creek that once spelt quarantined isolation to ships from the Levant. *Msida Creek* and *Pietà Creek*, where air-sea rescue and customs launches have their anchorage, are separated by Gwardamanġa Hill, crowned by St Luke's Hospital and the villa once occupied by Queen Elizabeth II.

We now steam out through the deeper open anchorage of MARSAMXETT HARBOUR beneath the fortifications first of Floriana and then of Valletta. The spire of the anglican *Cathedral* stands high above the cliff-like walls. To round *Fort St Elmo*, from the sea a formidable defence work, we briefly emerge into the open sea, then through the small boat passage in the breakwater enter ****Grand Harbour.** The damage done by the suicidal Italian attack of 1941 is still prominent.

We range the E. defences of Valletta, above which in succession slide past the *Sacred Infirmary* of the Knights, *Lower Barracca Gardens*, with the classical temple that is Sir Alexander Ball's memorial, and *Upper Barracca Gardens*. At water level are the attractive wharves of the Marina, the *Custom House* conspicuously graceful among the 17–18C store houses. The dome of *Ta Liesse* immediately draws the eye. The knightly wharves continue below the E. defences of Floriana, followed by the berths of the daily passenger ships to Syracuse and of the schools' cruising liners. *Marsa Creek* has commercial moorings and modern warehouses.

We turn back along the indented E. shore of Grand Harbour. *Corradino Heights* rise to the right above partly derelict remains of the coaling and oiling facilities that once served the Mediterranean fleet. The floating dock was built in Bombay and towed through the Suez Canal to replace an earlier one sunk by Italian aircraft in 1942. FRENCH CREEK, with the entrances to four graving docks, once rang to the noise of the repair shops of the Royal Navy. Now

merchant repairs and conversions are effected. The famous vedette carved with an eye and an ear is prominent as we round the peninsula of *Senglea* into DOCKYARD CREEK, where to huge caissons the Royal Navy moor a flotilla of destroyers or frigates in line ahead. Behind rise the cramped streets of Cospicua. *Fort St Angelo* on the point of Vittoriosa flies the admiral's pennant and proudly turns an impregnable face to the water. Between its base and the Senglea vedette stretched the great chain of the Siege.

Kalkara Creek and *Rinella Creek* are separated by Mt Salvator, the modest height on which the *Bighi Hospital* displays its elegant classical façade. In this section of the harbour large tankers are generally moored off the storage tanks that partly occupy the derelict defence works of *Fort Ricasoli*. Fort St Elmo rises again over the bows as the steamer recrosses the bar for the return to Marsamxett.

4 THE THREE CITIES

ROAD, not recommended on foot. BUSES (pea green) every 10 min. The direct approach across Grand Harbour may be made by dghaisa (price by bargain) to Senglea (Marina St.) or Vittoriosa (St Lawrence landing-place).

We take the main road out of Valletta and, beyond the Porte des Bombes, descend to (1 m.) *Mile End*, where the Hamrun road (Rte 8) leaves our road by an underpass. At *Marsa* roundabout we turn left, then take the right fork to pass round the industrial wharves of Marsa Creek. The road runs inland of Corradino Heights (comp. below) to (2¼ m.) a roundabout. To the left rises the direct road to Cospicua (by which we return; comp. below). We continue into the N. end of Paola (comp. Rte 5) and out to the E. on the Żabbar road.—Beyond (3¾ m.) *Fgura*, we pass the severe *Hompesch Arch* (1798) and, making a wide curve toward the N. avoiding Żabbar, approach the Cotonera Lines.

The THREE CITIES, all older in foundation than Valletta, were renamed after the Great Seige. They comprise Vittoriosa (Birgù), Senglea (L-Isla) and Cospicua (Bormla). Throughout the 17C, in the face of a series of threatened and attempted invasions, their defences were strengthened. The Floriana outworks (Rte 1B) were barely started when Francesco Firenzuola, summoned to review the defence works in 1638, warned that an enemy investing the hill of St Margherita, just E. of Vittoriosa, would command the entrance to Grand Harbour and be able to blockade the three cities. To incorporate both the hill and Cospicua, the **Margherita Lines,** designed by Firenzuola, were begun forthwith and three of the planned six bastions shortly finished. The remainder was not completed until 1716–36. In 1641 the Turks ravaged Gozo and effected a brief landing in Malta itself; there was a further scare in 1645. When Candia fell in 1669, invasion again seemed imminent. Nicholas Cotoner invited Maurizio Valperga to complete the works with a more comprehensive scheme. The **Cotonera Lines**, consisting of a semicircular ring of eight bastions and two semi-bastions, with a circumference of three miles and capable of sheltering 40,000 people with their livestock, were constructed in 1670–80. Owing to lack of funds the ravelins which should have guarded each curtain were never built. Much costly repair work was effected in the first half of the 19C, but as early as 1831 some bastions were in civil hands as dwellings.

Between massive bastions rises the ŻABBAR GATE, round which traffic now passes through arches pierced in the curtain wall. The gate bears an inscription recording the gift of the works by Cotoner. Beneath its great arch the iron bars that held the doors are still in place.

The space between the outer (Cotonera) and inner (Margherita) fortifications is adapted to various uses; though possessing its full quota of 'eyesores', it is of considerable interest to the student of military architecture and in parts not without a certain charm. The most interesting points can be explored on foot in 1–2 hrs and the road within the walls, though poor in the s. section, is negotiable by car.

Just within the gate (r.) St Edward's St. leads past *St Edward's College*, a boys' boarding school on St James's Bastion, and overlooks (l.) the huge buildings of *De La Salle College*, the boys' school of the Christian Brothers. It then skirts an attractive little cemetery, planted with cypresses. St Louis Bastion, behind, preserves its rampart walk (view). Beyond St Saviour's Bastion the road joins the Kalkara road (comp. below).

Returning to the Żabbar Gate we take Cotonera Road towards the Rock Gate entrance to **Cospicua** below the grim disused mass of *Verdala Barracks* (1853). This gate is little used since the modern Silver Jubilee Road skirts the inner defences to join St Edward's St. at the entrance to Vittoriosa (see below). If we turn left outside Rock Gate, taking the road which winds beneath high walls under the Margherita Bastion, we pass *Verdala Royal Naval School* and emerge in a plantation of trees below the old married quarters on St Nicholas Bastion. Beyond, a minor road from Fgura enters the lines by the impressive *Polverista Gate*, its upper part for many years in popular occupation. From it Blessed Virgin St. leads through the Margherita Lines into Cospicua proper.

The road between the defences continues past St John Bastion and *Valperga Bastion* (view of Docks) to descend to Għajn Dwieli Road (comp. p. 89).

We enter Cospicua by *St Helen Gate*, whence New St. leads directly to the central Gavino Gulia Square, outside the s. gate of the Dockyard. A good view of No. 1 Dock is obtained from the steps ascending to the parish church of the *Immaculate Conception*. The greater part of Cospicua is comprised of narrow streets and alleys rising in steps. St Theresa's St. skirts the hill along the dockyard wall to reach the modern St Margaret's Square, the bus terminus outside Vittoriosa. *St Margherita's Convent* is prominent to the right.

VITTORIOSA occupies the narrowing peninsula between Dockyard and Kalkara Creeks that ends in the Fortress of St Angelo. In medieval times, as *il Borgo del Castello*, or in Maltese **Birgu**, it was the principal centre of population on Grand Harbour, while the creek to the s. was the Port of Galleys of the Arabs. During the Sicilian régime it was the seat of the governor and until 1436 it shared with Mdina the ecclesiastical division of the island into two parishes. The Knights made it their residence in 1530. As in Rhodes they equipped themselves with a headquarters, or Auberge, for each Langue; but monastic seclusion in a Collachium (or inner city) was abandoned, though at least four of the auberges formed a compact central group. The city was dubbed Vittoriosa after the raising of the Great Siege, but the Knights moved to Valletta. Though the town suffered grievously in the Second World War, it retains some monuments from the period of the Order.

During the *Great Siege* of 1565, after the fall of St Elmo, the Turks turned all their forces against Birgu and Senglea. The two peninsulas and the harbour between were fortified as an entity. Across the harbour mouth was extended the great chain expressly forged in Venice. The inland defensive works opposed two short fronts towards the mainland and rapid communication between the two was assured by a bridge of boats. Just after St Elmo fell a small relief force from Sicily—the 'piccolo soccorso'—had successfully reached Birgu under cover of a sea mist. The first attacks in July fell upon the s. shore of Senglea where the Turks were engaged by Maltese swimmers on the improvised palisades. Hassem, viceroy of Algiers and Dragut's son-in-law. next led a land assault while his lieutenant Candelissa attacked from Marsa with a fleet dragged overland from Marsamxett. A squadron attempting to land Janissaries near the chain was blown out of the water by St Angelo's guns. The later attacks of August fell mainly against Birgu, where efforts were made by mining and with siege towers to invest the Castile bastion. At no time did the Knights retire to St Angelo, nor were the archives or the sacred relics in the conventual church taken to safety.

The present entrance to Vittoriosa is by Boffa Road. On foot, however, it is more interesting to take Couvre Porte Road, a little lower down the hill, pass through the *Advanced Gate* (1722), with attractive sculptured trophies of arms, and, making a dog's leg through the *Couvre Porte* (1723) and the *Vittoriosa Gate* (1727), enter across the moat. The moat itself is approachable by steps and prettily laid out as the Coronation Garden between *St John's Cavalier* and *St James's Cavalier*.

On the right as we descend Main Gate St. stands the **Inquisitor's Palace** (Pl. 1), or *Palazzo del Sant' Uffizio*, built towards the end of the 16C round the interior court belonging to the Castellania (1530). The palace has recently been restored and opened to the public (adm. see p. 47; ring bell).

The Inquisition, or Holy Office, the papal instrument for the sup-pression of heresy, was established in Malta in 1562, though the first nquisitor seems not to have arrived until after the Great Siege. The ffice was abolished by the French in 1798. In the 19C the building was used as officers' quarters.

The audience and residential rooms have been furnished with pictures and pieces of no great merit that do not belong to the building; but the timber ceilings are notable, and the coats-of-arms of various inquisitors that decorate the rooms include two who became pope: Fabio Chigi (1599–1661; Alexander VII) and Antonio Pignatelli (1615–89; Innocent XII). Beneath **are** the prisons.

From the irregular VICTORY SQUARE, farther on, Britannia St. leads to a group of buildings dating from before 1565. On the left he *Auberge of France* (Pl. 2), with a portal by Bart. Genga, faces Mistral St., where in succession on the left stand the *Auberge of Provence and Auvergne* (Pl. 3), Sir Oliver Starkey's House, and the *Auberge of England* (Pl. 4). In North St., farther on, is the *Auberge of Castile* (Pl. 5). A convent of Benedictine nuns occupies the first *Hospital of the Knights;* their church of *St Scholastica* has an altar-piece by Preti. The town walls, behind the convent, command Kalkara Creek. Old Prison St. ends by the ancient *Granaries* in steps that descend to the *Auberge of Italy* (Pl. 6). We return along St Lawrence St. which runs the full length of the town, but is cut off from Dockyard Creek by the high wall surrounding the naval purlieus.

St Lawrence, founded in the days of Roger of Sicily, and taken over by the Knights as their conventual church in 1530–71, was almost completely rebuilt to the designs of Lor. Gafà in 1691. The dome was ruined in 1942. The treasury contains a silver pro-cessional cross (carried round the streets on 10 Aug.) and relics brought from Rhodes. The *Oratory of St Joseph*, in the little square outside the N. door, preserves the hat and sword worn by La Vallette at the victory ceremonies in 1565.

A little to one side of the façade, steps lead down to the water-front here unencumbered since the Marine Gate and part of the curtain were destroyed by a powder explosion in 1806. To the right is the main gate (no adm.; but comp. below) to H.M.S. St Angelo. Just within, but better seen from the Senglea waterfront, is the monumental *Steam Bakery*, designed for the fleet by Scamp, with a clock tower inspired by that of Rennie's Victualling Yard at Devonport. The building was damaged in the bombing.

*Fort St Angelo, perhaps the symbol par excellence of the island's history, headquarters of the defending garrison throughout both sieges, still proudly flies the flag of the C.-in-C. Mediter-

The Three Cities

0   400   Yards
0   400   Metres

ranean, and is open to the public only on 7 and 8 September. The main entrance is reached from Dockyard Creek (comp. above), but on open days the best approach is by dghaisa from Valletta.

History. A pagan temple occupied the site probably from Phoenician times and its Roman successor may have survived until, in the 9C the Saracens built their first castle here. Count Roger built a small church dedicated to the B.V.M. in 1090. The name St Angelo may derive from Angelo de Melfi who held the islands as his fief in 1352–53. The castle passed in 1430 to the de Nava family, who built a palace within the citadel and added the chapel of St Anne. In 1530 the Grand Master made it his residence, and here in 1531 during his absence in Mdina the Turkish slaves mutinied. Four 16C grand masters were originally buried in the crypt of St Anne: de l'Isle Adam, del Ponte, de Homedes, and Claude de la Sengle. The fortress bore the brunt of the Turkish attack after the fall of St Elmo during the Great Siege. The Grand Master moved out in 1571 and St Angelo had a governor. La Cassière was imprisoned here after his deposition for rashly attempting to curb the licentious behaviour of his Knights. The fortress was repaired and altered in 1687–90 by Don Carlos Grunenberg.

Under British rule the fortress became the headquarters of the commandant of the garrison, until in 1912 the Admiralty took it over as *H.M.S. Egmont* to replace the old base ship of the Mediterranean fleet (Hibernia, renamed Egmont 1904) which had been moored at its foot. As headquarters of the C.-in-C. Mediterranean, the fort became *H.M.S. St Angelo* in 1933, and in 1935 the chapel of St Anne, which had been used as a store since 1798, was rededicated as the ship's chapel. Damage was done by sixty-nine direct hits in the bombing of 1940–43, when the slave tunnels were enlarged and used.

Senglea, approached from Gavino Ġulia Square by Mons. Panzavecchia St., suffered badly in the war and has few monuments of note. It was fortified by Claude de la Sengle in 1554. Fort St Michael, scene of fierce defence in 1565, was dismantled in 1922 and the stone used for a school. Marina St. affords the best view of Dockyard Creek. On Isola Point a small *Public Garden* on the ramparts affords the finest *Views of Valletta and of Grand Harbour. At the end is a celebrated vedette decorated with sculptured reliefs of an eye and an ear. Below are traces of the attachments of the Great Chain that guarded the harbour in 1565.

The **Docks,** formerly *H.M. Dockyard*, were relinquished by the Royal Navy in 1959 and converted to commercial use. The five graving docks have been enlarged to afford facilities for all types of repair to ships of up to 100,000 tons, but industrial disputes have delayed success and endangered the future of the yard. The first dock was opened in 1858. After 1865 the Royal Navy took over French Creek, the mercantile installations of which were moved to Marsa. The arrangements are in some ways reminiscent of those at Devonport, though the architecture is less distinguished. The Dockyard is completely isolated by a boundary wall, within which a separate complex of roads is approached through guarded gates. Connection between Dockyard Creek and French Creek is made by two tunnels through the base of Senglea under Panzavecchia St., and the complex includes the whole of *Corradino*

Heights where the principal depots were situated. Fortifications were erected in 1875.

The most direct return to Paola or Valletta is by GHAIN DWIELI ROAD which passes through the Valperga Bastion by a tunnel. At the top of the hill Cospicua St. continues into Paola, while Kordin St. (r.) leads directly into Paola Hill above Marsa Creek. The scanty remains of the early trefoil *Kordin Temple* are in the grounds of the prominent Technical School (key from Valletta museum).

THE N.E. QUARTER OF THE ISLAND. From the Salvatore Gate outside Vittoriosa a short descent brings us to **Kalkara.** KALKARA CREEK, once called English Creek when it was the anchorage for galleys of the langue of England, is now no more than a haven for dgħaisas, which are often to be seen beached for repair below the horn work of Castile. Rnella St. crosses the steep little peninsula of BIGHI, occupied by the **Royal Naval Hospital,** whose classical proportions make such an attractive contribution to the view from Valletta. The central building began its existence as the villa of Giovanni Bichi, grand prior of Capua, who retired to the then bare Mt. Salvator from his position as Master of the Galleys. Both Napoleon and Nelson used the villa as a military hospital. The edifice was completed with the flanking wings c. 1840 by Gaetano Xerri.

Rounding Rinella Creek we turn a sharp bend, leaving to the left *Fort Ricasoli*, now derelict and partly occupied for oil storage. The fort, which derives name from Fra Giov. Fr. Ricasoli who paid for it, was designed by Valperga·and begun in 1670 to replace a tower of 1629. During the siege a Turkish battery had occupied the point. The fort was the scene in 1807 of the mutiny of 'Froburg's Levy', when the mutineers blew up the powder magazine. In 1821 great breaches were made by the great storm of 8 February.

Behind Kalkara are the Capuchin monastery of Il Wileġ and a Naval Cemetery, from which narrow lanes wind through smallholdings above a fortified coast to *Marsaskala* (Rte 5).

5 VALLETTA TO ŻEJTUN AND MARSAXLOKK

Hal Saflieni, Tarxien, Tas Silġ

ROAD, bus (red with green stripe) from Castile Place, every 30 min., less frequently beyond Żejtun in winter.

Leaving Floriana, we take the Marsa road. At Marsa roundabout (comp. Rte 4) we may keep left and by Paola Hill enter Paola from the N., passing (l.) the huge Kordin Prison. Alternatively we may round the E. end of the racecourse and follow the Paola signposts at the next roundabout. On a hill to the right stands the attractive Victorian gothic chapel (1869) of the *Addolorata Cemetery*. Its memorial tombs, shrines, and chapels have the architectural elaboration familiar in Italy.

PAOLA or **Pawla,** a growing residential town (12,000 inhab.) with broad streets on a grid plan, is situated little more than a mile from the civil port and dockyard. It has a number of developing light industries and its s.e. extremities extend to the village of Tarxien (comp. below). From the square in front of the modern church of Christ the King we continue s. and leave the Tarxien road on our left. In Burials St. (r.) is the ***Hal Saflieni Hypogeum,** the most remarkable of Malta's prehistoric monuments. A labyrinthine subterranean sanctuary, discovered by accident in 1902 by workmen digging a well, it was cleared and systematically explored by Sir Themistocles Zammit. The modern entrance building contains show-cases of objects found during the excavations. It is likely that the function of the Hypogeum altered at some time from that of oracular temple to burial-place, for many thousands of human skeletons were found together with pottery and personal ornaments. A radio-carbon date obtained in 1967 shows that the place was in use c. 2450 B.C. The visit is habitually guided.

The Hypogeum into which we descend by a modern spiral staircase is on several levels. The uppermost level may have been natural caves which first suggested occupation, but the lower levels were hewn out and fashioned with the most sophisticated architectural features. Most striking are the main hall and the so-called 'holy of holies', both given concave façades simulating trilithon doorways, windows, and corbelled vaults; the oracle room with an echo chamber of impressively supernatural effect; and a deep chamber approached by an interrupted flight of steps with possibly sinister implication. Some chambers have remnants of decoration in red or black pigments, including the outline of a bull, and incised representations of hands.

From the Hypogeum the quickest way on foot to the Tarxien temples (500 yds) is to turn back towards the church; Sammat St., the second turning on the right, leads directly to Old Temples St.

TARXIEN, an agricultural village of narrow streets and tiny alleys, is famous for its **Temples,** excavated by Sir T. Zammit in 1914–19. Until the exploration of Skorba in 1961–63 Tarxien remained the only major megalithic monument in Malta to receive detailed publication after systematic digging. Though the largest and the most developed of the prehistoric remains in the islands, the Tarxien group of temples is less immediately striking than Ħaġar Qim (Rte 7) with its restored façade or Ġgantija with its more open position. Tarxien comprises three temples of different date but basically similar plan; as each later edifice was completed, the earlier structures became subordinate parts of the new. Presumably

Tarxien

FIRST
TEMPLE

M

K

SECOND

J

L

G

TEMPLE

H

F

E

THIRD TEMPLE

C

D

B

Main
Entrance

A

Cistern

space was the requirement since the archaeological evidence proves that the whole complex continued in use until its common end. Some of the more important features (altars, etc.) have been removed to Valletta museum and replaced by replicas.

We approach the latest or **Third Temple** from a semicircular fore-court. The main entrance is marked by a huge convex threshold (Pl. A); the façade walls are now represented only by fallen fragments extending for c. 50 ft to either side, though its former extent is clear. To the right the façade ends in a square structure (Pl. B); a huge stone block has six conical pits cut deeply in its surface and a large number of small stone balls were found in heaps near by. Possibly some form of divination by numbers was involved. The numerous large stone balls visible at many points were used as rollers in the transport of stone blocks.

Within the entrance a passage, paved with a single block, opens into a paved square space (Pl. C) surrounded by stone benches decorated in relief with spiral patterns. In the centre a circular patch of burnt floor shows the location of a sacrificial fire. Near by a stone basin with pitted decoration probably held ritual water. On the right stands an elaborate altar and in the apse behind are the remains of a colossal draped stone idol (originals, see p. 57). Here also were found cinerary urns and artefacts now in Valletta museum. On the left, by a secondary altar with relief carving, a narrow entrance opens into an apsidal chamber (Pl. D), much ruined, where were found sections of a frieze (copies in situ near floor level). The many niches found in the temple contained half-burnt bones, horns, or skulls of oxen, sheep, goats, and pigs, the same animals as are depicted in stone.

The main passage leads to the inner shrine where a huge decorated block fronts a platform supporting a framed trilithon (Pl. E). The apse to the left has a floor of torba and a small shrine flanked by pitted slabs.

To the right a triangular space (architecturally a seemingly clumsy link) brings us to the imposing entrance to the **Second Temple.** Its main passage (Pl. F) is paved and the wall blocks are pierced with holes where doors were attached by rope or leather hinges and secured by bars. We reach another paved square (Pl. G) with a circular hearth, perhaps the most suggestive part of the remains. Large apses open to either side and the whole should be imagined with a domed roof, which probably collapsed after an earthquake. In the w. apse is a monolithic stone bowl, restored after damage by vandals in 1925. The E. apse (Pl. H) leads to the First Temple (comp. below); off its s. side opens a room decorated with relief slabs of two bulls and of a sow suckling piglets.

The INNER APSES of the Second Temple were probably reserved to initiates or the priesthood since passage is impeded by an

laborately decorated slab. Beyond, a corridor extends between
tone benches. These support screens carved with spiral ornament
•n a pitted background with traces of red paint. To right and left
pses of especially well fitting upright slabs flank a central space with
. hearth (Pl. J) similar to that in the Third Temple only smaller. A
tone water basin stands in the left apse; between it and the wall
vas found the great terracotta bowl now in the museum at Valletta.
A further fine threshold leads into the final pair of apses, where
hat to the left (Pl. K) preserves one of the curved stones that
ormed the base of the dome.

Returning to the main elliptical space (comp. above) we ascend
wo steps to the **First Temple,** altered when the second temple was
dded. A secret stair (Pl. L), to the left, fashioned in the reduced
√. apse, by-passed this entrance. The innermost room (Pl. M) has
ie remains of a small chamber from which an 'oracle' spoke
irough a concealed hole in the wall.

Enormous blocks remain of the boundary wall that once enclosed
ie temple group.

The bus runs s.e. from Tarxien to the crossroads of *Bir id-Deheb,*
•here it turns left.—5¼ m. ŻEJTUN, an old agricultural village
‖1,500 inhab.), one of the parishes created in 1436, was formerly
ie administrative centre of the s.e. corner of the island. It was
icked in a Turkish raid of 1614. Our Lady of Mercy St. and its
arrow continuations lead to the centre, an irregular square in the
iadow of the parish church. Dedicated to *St Catherine,* this was
egun by Gafà in 1692 and has the usual solidity of his work, the
orizontal line being emphasized all round the building by massive
ornices, while the vertical line is also strongly marked by super-
iposed buttresses, of Doric inspiration below and Ionic above.
he dome is perhaps the most elegant part of the composition. St
regory's St. leads s.e. to the old parish church of **St Gregory,**
egun in 1436 and enlarged after the arrival of the Knights with a
assive but unfinished transept, surmounted by a low dome set
oon a drum.

The simple façade was embellished with a Renaissance portal and a
•llcot in the mid 16C. The tiny nave, of four bays, is buttressed ex-
rnally, an unusual feature in a Maltese church. The original church is
‖ but swamped by the Knights' transept, whose corner pilasters rise
om a plinth but are left in the air at an unfinished roof level.
From Żejtun a road leads e. in 3 m. to Marsaskala (comp. below).
i foot we may shorten the journey by branching left after 1 m.,
issing the little church of *Tal Ingrau* (or Ta' Ingraw; 1597).

Beyond Bir id-Deheb the road divides and we take the left
anch (to the right, see Rte 6), shortly joining a narrow by-road
iding directly from Żejtun.—6 m. **Marsaxlokk,** or *Marsascirocco,*
■ the e. arm of the bay of the same name, is the largest fishing
‖lage (1550 inhab.) of the island. The huge bay offers the easiest

sheltered landing; here both Piali in 1565 and Napoleon in 179£ disembarked their forces.

FROM MARSAXLOKK TO MARSASKALA is a rural walk of 3¼ m. A by-road runs E. from behind the sea-front to TAS SILĠ (¾ m.) where on a hill next to a Carmelite monastery, Italian excavators ir 1963–64 uncovered a Punico-Roman temple. Vases dedicated to Tanit and Hera and a Punic inscription in stone to Astarte sugges' that this is the celebrated *Sanctuary of Juno* plundered by Verres (a: Cicero records). In 1966 remains of a Christian baptistery were found. To the S.E. a long peninsula runs out to Delinara Point.— Tracks continue E. of Tas Silġ battery to *Xrobb il-Għaġin* (1½ m.) a headland on the base of which are vestiges of a Copper Age temple

Hence a track leads round *St Thomas Bay* to join the by-road from Żejtun (comp. above) just E. of the unusual *Mamo Towe* (17C), built on a saltire plan with a circular central chamber.— 3¼ m. **Marsaskala**, on a narrow sheltered inlet, is another fishing settlement. In the bay a small Turkish force came ashore in 161< and ravaged Żejtun, after which *St Thomas Tower* was erected or the headland to the s. to guard the landfall.

From Marsaskala (infrequent bus) we may return by an uninterestin road in a shallow valley via (2 m.) **Zabbar**, a town (11,050) whic! grew up in the 17C after the danger from piratical raids had diminishec From Żabbar via Paola to (6½ m.) Valletta, see Rte 4.

6   VALLETTA TO BIRŻEBBUĠA AND KALAFRAN.

Għar Dalam

ROAD, 7½ m.; buses (light blue with red and white stripe) every ½ h

We quit Valletta as in Rte 5 and take the new road by-passin Paola.—4½ m. *Bir id-Deheb* crossroads, see Rte 5. Leaving on ou left the road to Marsaxlokk, we continue s. with the valley c Wied Dalam on our right.

6 m. **Għar Dalam.** The entrance (signposted) is on the right c the road (adm. see p. 47; ring). We pass through the little museun and descend a long path to the cave. The natural CAVE, runnin into the lower Coralline limestone for 700 ft at right angles to th Wied, was worn by the action of water. Traces of stalagmites an stalactites are visible. The floor of the cave, when excavated i 1865 and 1892, proved to consist of five well-defined layers. At th bottom were three feet of sterile clay; above this three feet o bones, tusks and teeth, mostly of dwarf elephant and hippo potamus, welded into a solid mass by the action of water drippin through the limestone. Above this again, in five feet of red eartl were discovered bones and antlers of deer. The top layers, re pectively 15 in. and 9 in. in depth, represented detritus of th Neolithic and Bronze ages, and of the period since Phoenicia

times. The large number of animal remains is explained most plausibly by the theory that the cave became a swallow-hole, trapping both dead carcases and live animals. Restored skeletons of some of the species found are displayed in the *Museum*, together with bones from some 7000 animals. These seem to be all of European type, similar to those of the Pleistocene era identified in Sicily, suggesting that Malta may once have been joined to Europe but never to Africa.

From the cave mouth we look across the stony valley. On the opposing spur, but neither readily accessible nor very illuminating, are a Roman villa site, the remains of a Bronze Age village, and the temple known as *Borġ in-Nadur* after the name of the locality. Partially cleared in 1881, the area was properly excavated by Dr Margaret Murray in 1922–27. At the point where the main road touches the coast there are traces of 'cart ruts' leading into the sea.

—6½ m. *Birżebbuġa* stands on a headland separating St George's Bay from Pretty bay, two of the smaller inlets of the large landlocked Bay of Marsaxlokk. It has large oil storage facilities and a tanker jetty.—7½ m. *Kalafrana*, near the w. entrance to the bay, was once an important R.A.F. flying-boat base.

From the bottom of the hill below Għar Dalam a poor road (l.) continues E. round St George's Bay to *Fort St Lucian* (1610), still occupied by the military, then descends to *Marsaxlokk* (Rte 5).

From Kalafrana a minor road leads w. to *Żurrieq* (4 m.; Rte 7), passing round the Fleet Air Arm airfield of *Ħal Far*. Off the end of the S.E. runway 200 ft above the shore is *Għar Hasan*, a large cave (torch necessary) said to have been used by a Saracen hiding to avoid expulsion in 1120.

An alternative return (a mile or two longer) may be made by turning w. at Bir id-Deheb to *Għaxaq*, whence a bus runs via *Gudja*, birthplace of Gerolamo Cassar (1520–86), the architect, to *Luqa* (Rte 7), and thence to Valletta. At IX-XLEJLI, between Għaxaq and Gudja is the *Dorell Palace* (1770) where Bettina Muscati is said to have entertained in turn both Napoleon and Nelson. Midway between Gudja and Luqa, to the left of the road, stands the church of *St Mary Ta' Bir Miftuħ*, perhaps the best preserved of the parish churches built in 1436, through the settlement it served no longer exists.

7 VALLETTA TO ŻURRIEQ AND QRENDI

Haġar Qim and Mnajdra

ROAD, 6½ m.; Bus (orange) from Kingsgate.

The bus leaves the capital via *Marsa* (Rte 4), and skirts the S.E. corner of the Racecourse. Inside the track is the Polo Ground where Kipling's Maltese Cat had learned to be past pluperfect prestissimo player of the Game. We turn left. On the right is the huge hospital of St Vincent de Paule.—3¼ m. *Luqa* has given its name to the Airport which extends to the W. The church, begun in 1650, was almost destroyed in the Second World War. The altarpieces by Preti have been incorporated in the rebuilding. We leave the road to Gudja (Rte 6) on our left, and pass between Kirkop (l.) and Mqabba (r.; see below).

5½ m. **Żurrieq,** a long village of 7050 inhab., is one of the ten parishes of 1436. The parish church of St Catherine, begun in 1634, has been several times modified. It has a fine painting by Mattia Preti, who lived in the village during the plague of 1675. In the adjacent garden are some remains of the Punic and medieval periods. A near-by house is believed to incorporate much of a domestic building of Punic origin. The *Armeria*, a late 17C building, was used as an armoury during the grand-masterships of Pinto, Ximenes, and de Rohan, but became a private residence in 1784. The remains of a number of windmills date from the fifty years between 1674 and 1724 when the Order enjoyed a monopoly right to erect them.

About 1 m. to the W. lies **Qrendi,** to which the bus continues. A long main street runs almost N. and S. with the parish church off to the N.W. More interesting is the odd façade of *St Catherine Ta Torba* on the Mqabba road; plain blocks of masonry project from a recessed front to give a structural pattern. It was added in 1625 to an older nave. In Tower St. near St Saviour's, is the *Cavalier Tower*, the only tower on an octagonal plan in Malta. At the beginning of the Wied-iż-Żurrieq road is *Il-Maqluba* (literally 'turned upside down'), a depression 300 ft across and c. 150 ft deep, a geological vertical fault caused by the collapse of an underground cavern roof.

From Zurrieq or Qrendi minor roads descend to the coast at *Wied iż-Żurrieq*, frequented for underwater swimming. Here a boat may be hired (early morning best; 2/6 per person, minimum 4 persons) for a visit to the *Blue Grotto*, just to the E., a phenomenon similar to its better-known namesake in Capri.

The principal importance of Qrendi for the traveller lies in the two temple complexes situated to the s.w., the nearer of which is istant about 20 min. walk (signposts). **Haġar Qim,** the 'standing tones' were visible above the surface of the fields and suffered arly and unscientific excavation in 1839. The restoration of the nonumental façade, though somewhat crude at close range, gives :om a distance a striking impression of the scale of Maltese negalithic architecture. Here were found many of the steatopygous gurines, or fat divinities, now in the museum at Valletta.

In internal arrangement Haġar Qim differs considerably from •ther temples on the islands in that additions of radiating oval ooms have been made to an existing trefoil plan without any .ttempt at preserving an overall trefoil arrangement. An ancillary ntrance has been supplied at the back, another unusual feature.)therwise, the same detailed characteristics are found: the rope ioles, the roller stones, the apsidal arrangement, the pitted decora-ion, and the oracular chamber. The huge stone (23 ft by 9) near he N.E. wall rivals that at Ġgantija as the largest quarried block n Malta.

From the temple a path descends w. On the left stands a watch ower of the Order of St John. Nearby is a monument erected to ir Walter Congreve, governor in 1924–27, whose favourite spot his was. Six miles offshore lies *Filfla*, an uninhabited islet that has ong been used as a gunnery and bombing target by the Royal Navy and Royal Air Force. It has a unique species of lizard. The ath leads to another temple complex ⅓ m. away and some 125 ft ower.

*Mnajdra, comprising two temples, is less exposed to the weather han Haġar Qim and better protected by an outer wall of hard :oralline limestone. Although excavated early, it has suffered less ilteration and in its remote and unspoiled setting is one of the most beautiful of Maltese prehistoric monuments. The temples, set with heir axes at about 45 degrees, remain internally separate though aaving a common perimeter wall. The UPPER TEMPLE (r.) is entered by a port-hole slab within which an impressive vista opens through he inner entrance to the central apsidal shrine. To the left an inner :oom, also approached through a port-hole slab, has an altar.—The LOWER TEMPLE, probably older, has a more imposing en-:rance reached by steps. The usual trefoil plan has the addition of :wo rooms, fashioned either side of the short entrance passage between the façade and the main elliptical space. That to the right has a good torba floor, carved recesses and an oracular window. The main elliptical space has good pitted decoration and an exceptionally well-preserved trilithon entrance to the inner sanc-tuary.

In front of the temples and a little to the right is a small free-standing shrine. About 600 yds to the N.W. are six rock-hewn reservoirs of un-known date.

G

From Qrendi a short return may be made to the Zurrieq–Luq road via *Mqabba* amid a vast area of quarries. Alternatively w may continue N.W. to Siġġiewi (Rte 8).

8   VALLETTA TO ŻEBBUĠ AND SIĠĠIEWI

ROAD, 6 m.; bus (yellow) from Kingsgate to *Żebbuġ;* (yellow an red) to *Siġġiewi.*

From Floriana we take the middle road and just short of th centre of Hamrun (comp. Rte 9) fork left.

2½ m. **Qormi** (14,300 inhab.) created a parish in 1436, used to b called *Casal Fornaro* from its many bakeries. It has a confusin, medieval lack of plan with very narrow streets, and suffered mor than any place in the plague of 1813. The bus passes only throughl its southern outskirts. The High St. diverges to the right and ha some notable carved doorways and balconies. The *Stagno Palace* though in poor state, shows interesting details of its period (1589) The parish church of *St George* (1584) has a tall façade witl prominent w. towers; the dome is possibly a later addition.

Nearly 1 m. s. of the town lies *Tal Handaq*, where the Royal Nava College is maintained as a comprehensive school.

About ½ m. beyond the town we join the modern road which from Marsa, passes s. of the racecourse to bypass Qormi. At 3½ m the direct road to Siġġiewi (comp. below) diverges left. Just beyon the turn a small chapel marks the track (r.) leading to *Tas Hlas*, pretty church of 1690 amid the fields.—Just outside (4½ m.) **Żebbuġ** the road divides into three, the left branch, the old Main St. passing through *De Rohan Arch* (1677) into a maze of narrow streets Vehicles normally take the modern centre road, which enters the main square from the N. The town (8150 inhab.), once famous fo sail cloth made from locally grown cotton, is the birthplace of Dun Mikiel Xerri and Bp. F. X. Caruana, heroes of the revolt agains the French, as well as of Dun Karm, the national poet, and Ant Sciortino, the sculptor. *St Philip's*, the parish church, was built ir 1599. The façade is given added apparent height since its spar including the towers does not incorporate the aisles, neither are the aisle domes hidden by screens. The dome has a graceful lantern set upon an angular octagonal drum. Some of the houses beyond the E. end in Hospital Square are 350 years old.

The bus continues to (6 m.) **Siġġiewi**, an agricultural centre o 5250 inhab. amid fertile fields and farms. The parish church of *St Nicholas*, designed by Lorenzo Gafà in 1675–93, is perhaps the most spectacularly Baroque work on the island, though the arcaded w. portico was not added until 1864. The dome rides proudly on a high drum, and the high vault allows a flood of light to illuminate he ornament of the interior. The fine palace of the secretary of the Holy Inquisition survives.

About 1½ m. to the w. in the locality called *Ġirgenti*, on the s. side of the Wied Ix-Xagri, stands the *Inquisitor's Summer Palace* (no adm.), a well-proportioned if fortress-like house built by Onorato Visconti (1625–27) in a delightful situation. The little chapel of St Charles Borromeo was added in 1760.—Rabat lies 3 m. N.w. of Siggiewi.

Ghar Lapsi, 'the cave of the Ascension', a fishing inlet, lies at the foot of the cliffs just w. of Mnajdra (Rte 7) but is best approached from Siġġiewi, from which it is 2 m. by a winding country road ending in a steep hill.

9 VALLETTA TO MDINA (RABAT)

ROAD, 6 m.; bus (dark blue) from Kingsgate every 30 min.

Leaving Floriana, at Mile End (comp. Rte 4) we take the right fork to follow the long St Joseph's High Road through the busy centre of Ħamrun. Just N. of the central square on a site (Blata l-Bajda) once fortified against the French is a new student town. Here is preserved one of the locomotives of the former railway. In *Santa Venera*, now a w. extension of Ħamrun, we pass (r.) the 'Dar il-Lyuni', or *Casa Leoni*, a country villa built by Manoel de Vilhena in 1730. We cross the Birkirkara–Qormi road at Fleur de Lys roundabout and for the next 1½ m. follow the disused WIGNACOURT AQUEDUCT, built in 1610–14 to carry water to Valletta. It was originally 9½ m. long.—At 4 m. a by-road passes through its arches and crosses the bed of the former railway to reach **San Anton** (600 yds), now the principal residence of the Governor-General (no adm.). Built in 1625 as the country seat of Grand Master Antoine de Paule, who displeased the Inquisitor by the lavishness of his installation dinner here, it became the seat of the National Assembly from Feb. 1799 to the surrender of Valletta by the French in Sept. 1800. Here through the summer of 1810 ripened the romance of Lady Hester Stanhope and Michael Bruce, then on their way to the East. The attractive formal gardens are open free daily until sunset. San Anton forms part of Balzan (Rte 10B), though situated as near to

4¼ m. **Attard,** which lies just to the right of our road. Here the parish church of *St Mary*, built in 1613–16 by Tomasso Dingli, has been called the best Renaissance monument on the island. The large building, farther on (r.), is a hospital for mental diseases. We climb gently, then more steeply as the Qormi, Żebbuġ, and Siġġiewi roads come in one by one from the s., finally abruptly up Saqqajja Hill to the plateau (625 ft) on which stand (6 m.) Rabat and Mdina.

MDINA, *the* city par excellence as its name implies, was named by the Saracens when they reduced the compass of Roman Melita and refortified the citadel. In 1427 Alfonso V of Aragon dubbed it *Notabile* and the Knights called it *Città Vecchia* to distinguish it from their new city, Valletta. All three names still have currency and the walled city (850 inhab.) which rides the surrounding fields like a proud battleship dominates with its characteristic skyline the greater part of the island. Within the walls cloistered calm and harmonious buildings invoke its noble past. Outside the walls to the s.w. extends the untidy town of **Rabat,** a centre (12,600 inhab.) of the cottage lace industry and the market town for the w. half of the island.

Bus Terminal and CAR PARK just outside the Main Gate.

Hotels. Xara Palace (a), old-established; **Pointe de Vue** (b), on the Saqqajja.

Restaurants. *Birdcage, Barrel and Basket,* both in Rabat.

Post Office, Museum Road.

History. *Melita,* the Roman capital of the island, occupied nearly the area now covered by Rabat until, after A.D. 870, the Saracens reduced its compass to that of the present citadel of Mdina. Here in 1090 Roger of Normandy was hailed as liberator of the island. Alfonso the Magnanimous honoured the city in recognition of its citizens' redemption of the island for 30,000 florins from the Sicilian viceroy. Sinam Pasha's attack in 1551 was beaten off while the Maltese cavalry under Sir Thomas Upton harried the invaders in the plain below. In 1565 the city organized sorties against the Turkish camp at Marsa and later inhibited attack by reinforcing the walls with women disguised as soldiers, a ruse which deceived the enemy. After 1570 the city lost population to Valletta though Grand Master Martin Garzes tried to prevent this by granting special privileges to those who stayed. Here in 1798 the people rose against the French occupation.

Buses terminate on the SAQQAJJA, a broad esplanade with a fountain on the edge of Rabat and just outside the walls of Mdina. The outer line of fortifications has disappeared beneath modern approach roads and the pleasant *Howard Gardens,* planted with palms, citrus trees and Mediterranean pine. The existing enceinte consists of an irregular quadrilateral of medieval walls with four projecting bastions added by G. M. de Redin in 1657–60. As we approach we have a good view of the s. wall with its three bastions, *San Pietro* on the w., *de Redin* in the centre, and *del Palazzo* on the right.

A narrow bridge crosses the dry moat (first dug by the Arabs and now planted or laid out with handball courts). The site of an earlier drawbridge may be located by the outline of the former entrance, now blocked, in the wall 20 yds to the right. The present **Main Gate,** erected in 1724, bears an inscription and the arms of Manoel de Vilhena. On the inside the arms of Antonio de Inguanez continue to be displayed in accordance (as the plaque states) with the order of Alfonso V. The present escutcheon was placed in 1886, the original having been removed by the French in 1798.

Within the gate we are in St Publius Square, a narrow space having on the left the *Torre dello Standardo*, anciently the gate-house and now the police station. It dates from the early 16C; the Vilhena arms were added later. To the right the **Magisterial Palace,** built by Giov. Barbara for Vilhena, occupies three sides of an open courtyard which is closed by a screen and gateway. The principal façade has a fine doorway adorned with a portrait medallion of Vilhena in bronze. Used from 1860 until recently as the Connaught Hospital, the palace is being restored (1968) for use as a *Museum of Natural History and Folklore.*

We pass to the left of the massive walls enclosing the **Nunnery of St Benedict,** a closed order in strict seclusion whose members remain even after death in its own cemetery. The building dates from before 1418 but was altered in the 17C. On the corner as we reach Villegaignon St. is the little church of *St Agatha,* remodelled in 1694 to a design of Lorenzo Gafà, with an altarpiece by Gius. d'Arena. In the nunnery wall an inconspicuous portal marks the church of *St Peter,* which continues the dedication of the women's hospital that occupied the building before 1418. The altarpiece, Madonna with SS. Benedict, Peter, and Scholastica, is by Preti.

VILLEGAIGNON ST., the gently curving main street, is named after the French knight, Nicolas Durand de Villegagnon (c. 1510–71), who founded Nouvelle-Genève in Brazil (renamed after its capture by the Portuguese Rio de Janeiro) and (more relevantly) defended Mdina in 1551 against the Turkish attack. On the left a modern façade disguises the ancient *Casa Inguanez,* seat of the oldest Maltese family of title, created barons of Dyar-il-Bniet in 1350 and hereditary governors of Notabile before the arrival of the Knights. Here Alfonso V of Aragon stayed in 1432 and Alfonso XIII of Spain occupied the same room in 1927.

Facing the *Casa Testaferrata* (r.), seat of the Marquis of St Vincent Ferreri, are the 17C *Casa Viani* and the *House of Notary Bezzina,* once the offices of the Captain of the Rod. From its balcony the commander of the French garrison was thrown to his death on 2 Sept. 1798 by citizens infuriated by his auctioning tapestries looted from the Carmelite church. Farther on (r.) stands the beautiful *Banca Giuratale,* or Municipal Palace, built in 1730 by Vilhena when he appropriated the site of the older council house for his new palace (comp. above). It houses a girls' school.

The communes of Gozo and Malta were raised to municipal status by Roger of Normandy and had a form of local self-government. The Università (commune) had a consiglio populare, or council of jurats, elected from the heads of families. This had the right to appoint judges, to impose taxes, and to submit recommendations to the king. It reached its full development under Alfonso V. Among its officials were the Captain of the Rod, or chief magistrate, the four jurats, the Vice-Admiral, and the Secreto or tax-gatherer. In this building in Sept 1798, after the spontaneous uprising against the French commander the citizens declared a National Assembly and appointed Briffa to treat with Nelson against the French.

To the right opens ST PAUL'S SQUARE, its pleasing Renaissance harmony only disturbed by one unfortunate intrusion of Victorian gothic.

The **Cathedral,** dedicated to St Paul, a dignified Baroque building with a façade almost austere for its period, was rebuilt by Lor. Gafà in 1697–1702 after its Norman predecessor had been ruined by an earthquake in 1693. It occupies, by tradition, the site of the villa where St Paul converted Publius, chief man of the island, after curing his father of a fever.

A church probably stood on the site from the 4C, and this or a successor was rebuilt by Roger de Hauteville soon after 1090. The church has always been the see of a bishop, though before 1530 the titular bishop frequently did not reside in the island. The see became an archbishopric in 1797 and a metropolitan province in 1944. The two brass cannons in front of the façade were restored to Mdina in 1888 from the Artillery Museum at Woolwich.

The INTERIOR, in the form of a Latin cross, has aisle chapels hung during festivals with crimson damask, giving a rich and unifying effect to the whole. The nave and aisles are paved with variegated heraldic slabs commemorating members of the chapter and dignitaries of the church—the ecclesiastical counterpart of the pavement in St John's in Valletta. The ceiling is frescoed with scenes from the life of St Paul by Vinc. and Ant. Manno (1794). The marble font inside the w. door was presented by Bp. Giacomo Valguarnera in 1495 and survived the earthquake intact. The *Sacristy,* approached from the 3rd chapel on the left, is closed by carved *Doors of Irish bog oak saved from the w. front of the Norman cathedral. Opposite the door a monument commemorates Bp. Caruana, one of the leaders of the revolt against the French in 1798.

In the *N. Transept* a painting by Mattia Preti depicts the miraculous appearance of St Paul during the Saracen raid of 1422. The *Chapel of the Blessed Sacrament*, to the N. of the chancel, has a Byzantine ikon of the Madonna inevitably attributed to St Luke.

On the chancel arch the two medallions of SS Peter and Paul are not paintings but mosaics. The ceremonial plate used on the high altar during the patronal festival includes silver candlesticks, and a set of statues of the Virgin and the Apostles which belonged to the conventual church of St John and are attributed to Cellini. The *Stalls,* of marquetry, date from 1481, but the panels were replaced in 1876 by a craftsman from Floriana. The *Apse,* reconstructed in 1681 to receive Mattia Preti's fresco of the Shipwreck, withstood the earthquake.

The *Chapel of the Crucifix,* to the s. of the sanctuary, contains an interesting painting of St Paul, formerly the centre panel of a

Siculo-Catalan polyptych forming the main altarpiece of the church. The crucifix is by Fra Innocenzo da Petralla (17C). In the S. Aisle is buried Lord Strickland, prime minister of Malta in 1927–32.

Abutting the s. transept stands the *Archbishop's Palace* (1733), the official residence as opposed to the Curia which is in Valletta.

The **Cathedral Museum**, deriving from a bequest of works of art by Count Marchesi in 1833 and formerly housed in an annexe to the N. of the cathedral, is being transferred (1968) to the former *Seminary* opposite the s. door. Built in 1733 in a florid Baroque style of Sicilian inspiration, this building has a recessed centrepiece with a balcony supported in a seemingly casual manner by atlantes. The collections include the drawings and engravings of the original bequest, notably woodcuts by Dürer and engravings from them by Marcantonio Raimondi, engravings by Goya after Velasquez, and a drawing signed and dated 1581 by Luca Cambiaso. Among works that once adorned the cathedral are a Virgin at Prayer, by Sasso-ferrato, donated in 1687, panels from the 14C polyptych that once formed the main altarpiece (comp. above), and inlaid panels from the choir stalls by Parisio and Pierantonio Calatura of Catania. The vestments are specially interesting for fine specimens of ancient Maltese lace. The MSS include an early antiphonal. A portable altar decorated with Byzantine enamel work is said to have been used in the galleys of the Order, and a ceremonial Cross to have been carried into Jerusalem by Godfrey de Bouillon in 1099.

Recrossing the square, we return to Villegaignon St. The *Palazzo Santa Sofia*, on the left, displays a tablet of doubtful authenticity with the date 1233; the ground floor has, however, just claims to be the oldest building in Mdina. The upper floor was added in 1938. On the right is the tiny church of *St Roque*, popularly called 'Madonna tad-Dawl', which was removed here from the entrance gate during Vilhena's replanning operation. Almost opposite is the *Carmelite Church*, built after 1659 to the design of Fr. Sammut. The belfry was re-erected in 1857 after being thrown down the previous year by an earthquake. The confiscation of property from this church precipitated the revolt of 1798 against the French. The **Palazzo Falzon** (r.), often called the *Norman House*, is a good example of the Siculo-Norman style which survived almost to the coming of the Knights. The building may not be earlier than c. 1495 and is said to be the house occupied by de L'Isle Adam after his first arrival in Malta. The decorated double-lights were beauti-fully restored at the instance of Sir Harry Luke during his gover-ship. The corner house (Beaulieu), beyond, incorporates part of the Benedictine nunnery of Santa Scholastica, founded here in 1496 and moved in 1604 to Vittoriosa.

BASTION SQUARE, the former firing-platform at the N. point of the city, though exposed to the full force of northerly gales, makes a wonderful vantage point from which the *View is one of the finest in Malta. On the opposing ridge, across the Hemsija Valley, stand the David Bruce Military Hospital and the imposing cantonments of Mtarfa, given a focal point by a tall clock tower. Farther right in the middle distance the dome of Mosta rises from its hollow. In the distance, across the disused fighter airfield of Ta' Qali, stand out the fortifications round Grand Harbour. All round, amid a patchwork of stone-walled cultivated plots, the huge churches dominate their cream and golden villages. In every direction the distant sea borders the land. On a clear day Mt Etna's snow-capped crest in far off Sicily can be seen thrusting through its ring of cloud.

Bastions Street leads back shortly to the cathedral, passing *Casa Manduca*. Two other patrician houses (Depiro and Mifsud) are now linked by a bridge across the street and together house a girls' school. In the tiny square to the left is the entrance to a tunnel under De Redin Bastion by which the rebel Maltese forces penetrated the city in 1798.

The W. half of Mdina should be visited for its venerable calm and for the many exquisite details of its domestic architecture, such as window mouldings, brass knockers, and armorial bearings carved in high relief. Carmel St. leads to Magazines St. where the *Casa Isabella* has well-restored double lights. Behind the little chapel of *St Peter* (1617) runs a narrow lane where the medieval façades are lightened by delicate windows. From the church of *St Nicholas* it is possible to see through both the postern or *Gharreqin Gate* and the *Greek's Gate*, pierced in the oldest part of the walls, by which a road emerges through the moat into Rabat. MESQUITA ST., curving an unspoiled way across the city, is divided into three by the little Piazza Celsi and Villegaignon St. Off the centre section (l.) the *Gatto Murina Palace* has a fine 14C façade decorated with the lamprey motif of the family arms.

Turning right through the sombre St Paul's St. we reach a charming small square in front of the *Xara Palace*, formerly the seat of the Moscati-Parisio family and now a hotel. The foyer is adorned with vigorous bronzes by Sciortino. Opposite stands the *Corte Capitanale*, where figures of Mercy and Justice and the inscription 'Legibus et Armis' recall its former function of criminal court. Beneath there are still dungeons from an earlier building. It has for a long time shared the functions of the Vilhena Palace which it adjoins. The graceful loggia that closes the square in front of the E. rampart was the *Arengo* from which the town herald proclaimed the regulations of the Università or 'harangued' the citizens.

Quitting Mdina by either the main gate or Greeks Gate and recrossing Howard Gardens, we find ourselves in Museum Road. To the right is the **Roman Villa Museum** (adm. see p. 47), a misnomer, for the remains on which it stands are those of a town house rather than a villa. During the excavations of 1881 a number of mosaic floors were uncovered. Busts and heads of various emperors, sarcophagi, and inscriptions are displayed beneath a restored peristyle.

We enter **RABAT** by St Paul's St. which, passing Ta Doni and Ta Gesù churches, leads directly to the parish church. **St Paul's,** given its present form at the end of the 17C, seems to have been remodelled in order better to combine the earlier parish church of 1575 with a chapel of St Publius erected in 1617. The latter had been a work of piety of Giovanni Beneguas, who came from Cordova to join the Knights but instead lived as a hermit in the GROTTO OF ST PAUL, a cave now beneath the church (open 8.30–12, 1.30–6). This is locally venerated as either the 'dwelling' or the 'prison' of St Paul and credited with a miraculous propensity for staying the same size however much stone is removed from it.

Crossing an irregular square in front of the little chapel of St Cataldus, we take St Agatha's St. On the left is the entrance to **St Paul's Catacombs** (adm. see p. 47), an extensive system of passages and alcoves used as a burial place in the 4–5C. Farther on, to the right, are *St Agatha's Catacombs* (daily 8–6, 1/-), dedicated to a young girl who fled here from the persecutions of the Emp. Decius in Catania.

An avenue through St Paul's Churchyard leads into the narrow Main St. which we follow back to the Saqqajja. At the bottom of Saqqajja Hill the Siġġiewi road is known as Racecourse St. from the custom of racing horses and donkeys here on 29 June. The grandstand of the Grand Masters survives and the Mnarja races draw crowds from all over the island.

In St Augustine's St. the great *Augustinian Church*, designed by Cassar in 1571, has a gilded barrel vault. In Hospital St., to the left, adjacent to the Franciscan Convent, stands *Santo Spirito Hospital*, established before 1347 and still admitting patients. Behind, in the main road, is the *Saura Hospital* of the Sisters of Charity, founded in 1667 and occupying a commanding situation on the edge of the town.

Buskett Road leads S.E. past St Dominic's Priory (16C). About a mile outside the town stands *Verdala Castle (open Tues and Fri 9–1, 2–5), a summer palace designed for Grand Master Verdalle by Gerol. Cassar in 1586 in the form of a fortified medieval keep surrounded by a moat. Its halls and dungeons were used in 1812 to house French prisoners of war. Verdala, now the summer residence of the governor-general, is laid out with an elaborate garden and a 'Boschetto' of Aleppo pines and citrus trees. These shady *Buskett Gardens* (open daily) are a favourite retreat in summer.

A by-road turns w. to *Dingli*, the highest village on the island, situated a bare ½ m. from the tremendous *Cliffs that in this quarter drop 800 ft almost sheer into the sea. To the s.e. of Verdala, off a by-road to Siġġiewi, is Girgenti (Rte 8).

FROM RABAT TO MĠARR AND GHAIN TUFFIEHA, 6 m. We take the Mosta road and in the Wied Ta l'Isperanza turn left. The road passes over the gentle *Falka Gap* and crosses a fertile valley.— 3¾ m. *Zebbieħ.* At the police station is kept the key to the **Skorba Temples,** the scanty remains above ground excavated by David Trump in 1961–63. Here a temple of the usual trefoil plan has modifications of the Tarxien period; the complex was sacked and decayed before being used as a burial ground before the end of the Copper Age. The main discovery was of two superimposed hut settlements, characterized by the grey and red pottery wares which have taken the name of the site. These date from the 4M B.C. About 1 m. to the w. in the village of **Mġarr** are the *Ta' Haġrat* temples, with similar remains.—6 m. **Ghain Tuffieha** (*Golden Sands Hotel; Cote d' Or Hotel*), or *Golden Bay*, once a military camp and naval rifle range, is now frequented for its two beaches.

10   VALLETTA TO ST PAUL'S BAY AND MELLIEHA

A   By the Coast Road

BUSES, on Sun. aft. in summer only, from Manoel Island Bridge to St Paul's Bay.

To (6 m.) *St Julian's*, see Rte 2. We bear left and ascend the valley behind St George's Bay. On the right St Andrew's Barracks extend to *Pembroke Fort* (1878), a defensive work that takes name from Lord Herbert, secretary for war in 1855. To the left is the Roadside Inn restaurant. The steep hill (l.) crowned by *Madliena Fort* forms the N. end of the escarpment dividing the island (comp. below); a steep by-road climbs to Għargħur. Our road descends to the coast at 8¾ m.) *Baħar iċ-Ċagħaq Bay* (Palm Beach Rest.), then crosses the fortified Qrejten Point on which stands Qalet Marku Tower.

The *Għallis Tower* on the next headland is accessible and typical of many defensive structures built by the Knights. We round SALINA BAY (*Salina Bay Hotel*), where salt pans have been worked since the early days of the Knights. By the farther entrance to the hotel is a redoubt and interesting remains of a *Fougasse*, effectively a mortar hewn from the living rock and designed to decimate any force attempting a landing. At the head of the bay the *Kennedy Memorial Grove*, designed by Joseph Spiteri (1966), commemorates with dignified simplicity the murdered American president. Off the track behind the grove are some scanty remains of *Tal-Qadi Temple*.

At 12½ m. we join the road from Mosta, comp. below.—13 m. *St Paul's Bay*.

B Via Mosta

ROAD, 16 m. BUSES from Castile Place: to *Mellieħa* (white with pale blue stripe) with extensions to Marfa, Għain Tuffieħa, etc.; to *Mosta* (brown) every 10 min.; to *Naxxar* (brown with yellow stripe) every ½ hr.

From Valletta to *Msida*, see Rte 2. We keep straight on by Valley Road, passing (r.) an ancient wash-house still in use, and rising gradually in the Msida Valley.—3¼ m. **Birkirkara**, an old-established village (16,950 inhab.) of narrow streets, extends mainly to the N. of our road. *St Helena's*, a youthful work of Dom. Cachia, was built in 1727–45 in a rich Baroque which has earned it the description of 'the finest parish church on the island'. Externally the façade, the aisle screens, and the entablature are notable, while within the frescoes are striking. The ruinous old church of the *Annunciation* (1600), designed by Vitt. Cassar, lies to the left of the main road near the old railway station. Beyond the centre of the town we bear right and pass through the N. part of (4 m.) *Balzan*. Here the parish church has an unusual façade (1669) of Spanish inspiration. To our left lies the village of *Lija*.— At 5¼ m. the Naxxar bus turns right.

Naxxar, an ancient village (4800 inhab.) and a parish since 1436, is now isolated from the main routes across the island. From its commanding ridge the relief force of Ascanio de la Corna charged down on Mustapha's forces in the last battle of 8 Sept 1565. The modest dimensions and severe form of the parish church of *Our Lady of Victory* (1616) are disguised by an assertive façade, higher and wider than the nave, added with the aisles in 1912. A few yards from the bus terminus is the *Bird Museum* (9–12, 3–6; free but donations welcome) with a private collection of more than 600 birds. The grounds of the *Palazzo Parisio* have been since 1960 the venue of the Malta Trade Fair.

From Naxxar minor roads descend in every direction, one to the N.W. passing through the Victoria Lines (comp. below) by the Naxxar Gap to Salina Bay (3 m.). The bus continues N.E. to *Gharghur*, another high and isolated village (1850 inhab.), whence a winding and steep descent joins the coast road beneath the Madliena Fort (comp. above).

6¼ m. **Mosta** (7350 inhab.; Restaurants) is dominated by the huge *Dome of St Mary's*, a landmark from many parts of the island. The church was built in 1833–60 in imitation of the Roman Pantheon to the designs of Giorgio Grognet de Vassé, and the dome was erected without the use of scaffolding by notching each course to the one below. It is claimed to be the third largest in the world, exceeded in size only by St Peter's, Rome and St Sophia Istanbul.

A bomb which crashed through the dome while a service was in progress failed to explode and nobody was hurt.

Mosta is a good starting-point for walks along the **Victoria Lines,** a series of forts (1875–80) with supporting works along the escarpment caused by the *Great Fault.* This natural feature has always provided a tempting defensive line with the result that the unprotected N.W., despite its greater fertility, has remained sparsely populated. Minor roads follow virtually the full length of the ridge, and these and paths nearer the edge afford a series of wonderful views of the indented coastline.

The NORTHERN END (Mosta to Għargħur, 3 m.) may be reached by taking the St Paul's Bay road (comp. below) and beyond the bridge turning right. Leaving Fort Mosta on the left we recross the Wied Ta l'Isperanza and follow the Lines across the *Naxxar Gap* (p. 109) to Għargħur. Here a by-road leads along the flank of Ġebel San Pietru to a signal station overlooking Salina Bay. The principal road winds round a rocky gully to *Fort Madliena* (comp. above).

The SOUTHERN END (Mosta to Baħrija, c. 6 m.), where the ridge is more elevated, is further from habitation. At the *Targa Gap* on the St Paul's Bay road a by-road follows the ridge, crossing the Mosta–Għain Tuffieħa road in the *Falka Gap.* A long steep hill climbs w., then divides round the crest of the ridge. *Id-Dwejra* (680 ft.), a commanding situation, affords magnificent views down to Għain Tuffieħa, and on the s. side looks across the *Chadwick Lakes,* a series of reservoirs in the Wied Tal Qlejgħa, to Mtarfa. Beyond the *Binġemma Gap* the road rises again to the *Nadur Tower* (786 ft.), where there are good examples of prehistoric 'Cart-Tracks', then crosses the *Santi Gap.* This is here threaded by a road from Rabat, which descends N. past the remote and rocky *Gnejna Bay* to Għain Tuffieħa. To the s. of both of the roads that continue to the edge of the w. cliffs above Fom Ir-Riħ Bay lies *Baħrija,* a hamlet with a late Bronze age site.—On the return any of the roads branching off to the s. lead to Rabat.

We quit Mosta in a N.W. direction, cross Ta' l-Isperanza Valley by a bridge over the Wied il-Għasel, and descend abruptly through the *Targa Gap.* To the right Mosta Fort crowns an isolated rocky eminence; it has recently become the headquarters of Malta's civil defence force. At the hamlet of (8¾ m.) *Bur Marrad* we meet a by-road descending from Naxxar just inland of Salina Bay. On the lower slopes of Ġebel Għawżara, 350 yds to the s.w., stands the little 17C church of *San Pawl Milqi.* Here Italian excavations since 1963 have uncovered remains of three previous churches on the site. Adjacent were rediscovered remains of a Roman villa first noted in 1879, which flourished from 1C B.C. to 4C A.D., and was latterly used for the manufacture of oil. A well-head inscribed 'PAULUS' and a graffito depicting a wrecked ship attest the early association with this area of the landfall of the apostle.

Keeping right at Wardija crossroads, we soon join (9½ m.) the coast road (Rte 10A) half way between Salina Bay and St Paul's Bay. Here a by-road (r.) runs to the Qawra Tower, passing after another ¾ m. some remains near the shore of St Paul's Bay of a neolithic *Temple*, generally known as that of Buġibba (comp. below).

10 m. **St Paul's Bay**, more correctly *San Pawl il-Baħar* (2950 inhab.), extends for nearly a mile along the s. side of the bay from which the retreating forces of the Turks made a fighting re-embarkation in 1565. Its little harbour is guarded by the *Wignacourt Tower* (1610). Hardly a gap separates the houses from those of *Buġibba* to the E. Across the bay *St Paul's Islands*, really little more than rocks, are by tradition the site of the apostle's shipwreck in A.D. 60 (Acts xxviii, 7). The largest islet has the Maltese name of Selmunett and bears a statue of 1845.

Rounding the head of the bay we leave on our left a road through Pwales Valley to Għain Tuffieħa (2½ m.; Rte 9). A short sharp hill takes the road over the E. end of Bajda Ridge. On the long steep climb up Mellieħa Ridge (500 ft) a by-road (r.) gives access to SELMUN PALACE, now a hotel. This castle-palace, built by Dom. Cachia in the 18C on a plan deriving from the Verdala palace, was once the property of the Monte di Redenzione, a charitable foundation established by Father Rafael in 1607 to ransom Christian slaves from the Barbary coast.

13¼ m. **Mellieħa**, occupying a dominating position on its ridge, was made a parish in 1436 but abandoned before 1530 owing to Corsair raids. Its present plan dates from the agricultural colonization of the mid 19C, but its population (3950 inhab.) is again declining. The steep main street descends by corkscrew turns below the *Church*, which stands on a commanding spur above a rock-cut chapel of uncertain date.

In *Mellieħa Bay* (Seabank Hotel; Tunny Net Restaurant), with a shallow sandy beach, the relieving force of the Sicilian viceroy landed on 6 Sept 1565. The road here is sometimes flooded in winter. *Marfa Ridge*, surmounted by another steep approach, is guarded by the *Red Tower* on which an inscription records its erection in 1649. The ridge commands a fine view across the S. Comino Channel to Gozo.

Along the ridge a road runs E., from which six parallel roads at regular intervals descend to the Channel, serving various batteries and redoubts. This curious geometrical road plan is not military in origin, however, but part of a scheme of agricultural colonization of the 1840s.

The main road descends to the landing stage at (16 m.) *Marfa* (Rfmts.), whence the ferry plies to Gozo. To the E. stands the *Ramla Bay Hotel* and to the w. a road leads to *Paradise Bay* (1 m.), with another hotel and the alternative (bad weather) stage of the ferry.

GOZO

GOZO, in Maltese **Ghawdex,** the smaller main island of the
Maltese group, is separated from Malta by a channel some five
miles wide. Less fortified and less defensible, without a major
harbour to serve as a base, it has remained a backwater, too close
to have a distinct existence, suffering the sister island's misfortunes
but rarely sharing her prosperity and never her political importance.
Though the geological formation is the same, the outcrops are
different, so that Gozo has a number of bare flat-topped hills rising
above a more undulating landscape. The outcrops of blue clay are
more extensive, making the land more fertile, and Gozo's chief
rôle has been to supply agricultural produce to the more populous
island. Though half the size of Malta, Gozo has only one tenth of
the population. Fishing provides an alternative livelihood and, for
the women, the making by hand of the exquisite lace for which both
islands used to be famous. The Gozitans lead a serene and simple
life, the survival of which depends on whether they are visited by
those wanting relief from modern ways or those intent on intro-
ducing them. The principal attractions are the scenic walks. Gozo
has been called, not entirely without justification, the 'Ireland' of
Malta.

History. That *Gozo* has always had direct connection with Maltese
culture is shown by the similarity of the Ġgantija temples to those of
Tarxien and Haġar Qim. In general the history of the two islands is
indissolubly linked. But even as early as the Bronze Age pottery styles
evolved with variations between the two islands. Both Malta and Gozo
had municipal status under the Romans, and the cultural differences
widened during the Saracen period when Gozo remained more largely
Christian than Malta. The Sicilians granted both islands a Università
(comp. p. 101) and there is no evidence that one was subservient to the
other. In 1551 the Turks invaded Gozo and thousands of the inhabitants
were carried off into slavery after the garrison capitulated. The island
was afterwards treated as a security risk, the office of Captain of the
Rod (or Hakem) abolished, and a governor appointed by the Grand
Master. Gozo was attacked by the Turks for the last time in 1708.

Gozo

⊞ Tower ⊟ Redoubt *Antiquity ‡Church

0 · · · · · · · 1 · · · · · · · 2 Miles
0 · · · · 1 · · · · 2 · · · · 3 Kilometres

Ramla
Bay

Calypso
Cave

San Blas
Bay

aghra

Qamlet
Qorrot

ntija

Nadur

Qala

Qala Point

North Comino Channel

Ghajnsielem

Mgarr

Fort Chambray

Mellieha
Point

COMINOTTO

Annunciation

COMINO

Ras l-Irqhieqa

South Comino Channel

MALTA

11 VALLETTA TO VICTORIA (RABAT)

Post-Bus, 3–5 times daily, from G.P.O., Merchants Street, Valletta, connecting with Marfa–Mġarr Ferry ($\frac{1}{2}$ hr crossing; 1/-), whence bus to Victoria. The steamer takes a limited number of cars for which early booking is advisable. It is possible to hire a car at Mġarr. In winter gales sometimes prevent the crossing.—*Comino* is reached by launches.

In summer a direct *Hydrofoil* plies between Grand Harbour (Custom House Pier) and Mġarr or Marsalforn (excursion only; baggage not accepted); and those who prefer a longer voyage can sometimes obtain passage on the regular freighters that follow the same course.

The bus follows the inland road through Attard (comp. Rte 10B) to *Marfa*; from Sliema it is shorter by private car to follow the coast road (Rte 10A). The steamer leaves from Marfa except in bad weather when it may use a more sheltered bay farther w. We pass to the s. of Comino, on which *St Mary's Tower* (1618), built by Alof de Wignacourt, commands the South Comino Channel (Il-Fliegu ta' Malta). Here, off the s.e. coast of Comino, H.M.S. *Sultan* was wrecked in 1889.

COMINO, or *Kemmuna*, a rocky island (1 sq. m.) of Upper Coralline limestone, supports less than 30 inhab. on scattered farms, but is frequented for its good bathing. Here, between 1285 and 1291 Abraham ben Samuel Abulafia, the Jewish sage from Saragossa, wrote his best known prophetic work. *Santa Marija Bay*, on the N. coast, above which stands the little church, has a fine sandy beach with the Club Nautico, while in the adjacent *San Niklaw Bay*, to the w., stands the Comino Hotel. The fractured s. coast, off which lies the uninhabited islet of *Comminotto* (Kemmunett), has a picturesque lagoon popular with underwater enthusiasts.

Landfall on Gozo is made at **Mġarr,** the principal harbour of the island, generally full of gaily painted small boats. The little port is dominated by Our Lady of Lourdes, a modern church in an alien Gothic style, from which there is a fine view across the strait. To the s.w. rises a steep promontory crowned by *Fort Chambray*. Designed in 1723 by De Tigné as a fortified township to replace the Castello, it was not built until 1749–60 when the cost was defrayed by Jacques François de Chambray, a French knight who had achieved fame as commander of the galleys. The interior was laid out in square plots on the pattern of Valletta, but few of the plots were taken up and a town never materialized. The fort put up an unavailing resistance to the French in 1798 and was garrisoned for a time by British troops. Today it only shelters a hospital.

The road climbs up the valley to *Għainsielem*, almost contiguous with Mġarr, where a new convent of huge proportions is rising on a prominent spur. Beyond the village we pass Santa Ċilja Tower in an area cleared in twelve days in 1943 to make an airstrip for the invasion of Sicily. We cross the road from Qala (Rte 12) to *Xewkija*

(3050 inhab.), which lies to our left. Here a huge new church is wholly enveloping the old one. To the right Xagħra is prominent on its ridge.

3¾ m. **VICTORIA** (*Duke of Edinburgh Hotel*), named for the diamond jubilee of 1897, or **Rabat** as it is still generally known, is the little 'capital' (6300 inhab.) of Gozo. Both in its inland fortified position and in its twofold composition of citadel (Il-Kastell) and suburb, it resembles the old capital of Malta.

We enter by the broad RACECOURSE STREET, passing (l.) *Rundle Gardens*, where the annual agricultural show is held on 14–15 August. Beyond the Commissioner's Residence and the Marsalforn turning, we enter the old part of the town. On the left is the *Post Office*. IT-TOKK, the 'Main Square', with a monument to the fallen of the Second World War unveiled by Queen Elizabeth II, separates the citadel from the suburb. Here the Gozo Civic Council sits in the *Banca Giuratale*, erected (1733) by Vilhena for the Università. From *St. James's*, rebuilt in 1740, the crops are annually blest on the feast of St Mark (24 April).

The steep CASTLE HILL mounts (r.) to **Il-Kastell,** now entered by a broad modern archway, created since the Second World War. To the right is the old Entrance Gate adorned with a Roman inscription from a still earlier gate. From a confined piazza steps admit to the CATHEDRAL, designed by Lor. Gafà and built in 1697–1711. The church of the Assumption was raised to diocesan status in 1866. The three heraldic plums of Grand Master Perellos are prominent in its decoration. The font is of locally quarried alabaster. The trompe l'oeil painting in the dome is by Antonio Manuele. On the w. side of the square are the *Public Registry*, which before 1551 was the residence of the Ħakem of Gozo, and the *Law Courts*, erected by Wignacourt.

A small arch to the E. of the cathedral leads to the MUSEUM in the former Palazzo Bondi. On the ground floor are displayed agricultural implements and Roman remains from the island, among them a marble head of a boy and numerous amphorae recovered from a wrecked wine ship in Xlendi Bay. The upper floor, devoted to the prehistoric period, has finds from the excavations at Ġgantija, including objects connected with fertility rites, stone rollers, and pottery.

Turning right, we may reach the ramparts, which afford a marvellous *Panorama of the island. From this vantage-point the differences between the Gozo landscape and that of the sister island are very marked: from undulating fields rise sharp outcrops of rock on whose eroded tops ride the straggling villages. We pass the now disused *Prison* and come to a cavalier built by Alof de Wignacourt. A flight of steps mounts to the next rampart walk, commanding both the surrounding countryside and the ruined medieval buildings within the walls. Two Siculo-Norman houses survive in fair condition amid the encroaching prickly pear.

To XLENDI, 2 m. s. A steep hill descends into the narrow Xlendi Valley which ends in a pretty land-locked *Bay sheltering the fishing hamlet of **Xlendi**. A path round the s. side of the bay affords striking views of the vertical cliffs opposite, in which opens Carolina Cave. Underwater research has recently produced Roman remains from sunken galleys.

12 EXCURSIONS FROM VICTORIA

The bus services radiate from Rabat, but hardly anywhere on the island is out of reach of good walkers.

A To the Ġgantija and Marsalforn

BY-ROADS, affording a pleasant walk of c. 4 m., practicable by car.—Buses to *Marsalforn*, 3 or 4 times daily; more frequently to *Xaghra* (no connection between the two villages).

The uninteresting direct road to Marsalforn (2 m.) descends in a long valley, dominated from the N. by Il-Mirżuk, a conical hill with a concrete statue of the Saviour set in position by helicopter.

We take Racecourse Street, and after ¾ m. bear left and (1¼ m.) left again. On our left rises the irregular plateau on which stands the scattered village of **Xaghra,** the population of which (3600 inhab.) is declining. Where the main road to the village starts to zigzag uphill (l.) we continue straight by a by-road that climbs between the plateau and the isolated hill of Nuffara (probably occupied in the Bronze Age). We arrive shortly at (2 m.) the **Ġgantija,** in some ways the most impressive of all the Maltese Copper age temples, though the protective fence detracts from its commanding situation. The monument was fully uncovered as early as 1827. The complex comprises two temples, the main one to the left with a subsidiary structure (smaller and later) to the right.

The FAÇADE is remarkably well preserved, with a huge threshold slab. The usual pivot holes, hinge holes, and bolt holes are prominent, and some of the blocks are adorned with spirals or pitted decoration. Most impressive are the majestic proportions of the perimeter wall constructed of header and stretcher stones of gigantic size.

A path across the fields, or Parisot Street, slightly longer, leads to the centre of the village, prominently marked by its *Church*, whose only interest is in a recumbent figure under a side altar (l.), recalling those of the Sicilian folk plays. Near the church two small limestone caverns (Għar ta' Ninu and Għar ta' Xerri), each opening from a private dwelling, show the usual stalactite formations.

A more direct return to Victoria may be made by Church Street and its continuation Steep Street. As Xaghra Road this way joins the main Marsalforn road just below its junction with Racecourse Street.

A difficult descent on foot may be made from the village to Ramla Bay, better reached from Nadur (comp. below).

The roads either side of Xagħra church join as another Race-course Street, at the end of which the left fork begins the long descent (c. 2 m.) towards Marsalforn. On the way there are pleasant views of the valley (l.) with the prominent Tas Salvatur. On the ridge to the right wind pumps irrigate the fields.

Marsalforn (*Calypso Hotel; Starboard Club Hotel*), an attractive fishing village, borders a rocky bay in which a tiny harbour provides shelter from northerly gales. It is a popular summer resort of Maltese from the towns and abroad, but in winter many of its cottages turn a shuttered front to the sea.

An unmade road passes salt pans on its course round the coast w. toward *Żebbuġ* (1½ m.), a village (1200 inhab.) occupying a steep and picturesque ridge (413 ft) running N. and s.

B To Nadur and Calypso's Cave

We take the same road but keep right at the second fork, climbing on to the ridge occupied by (3 m.) Nadur, a small town of 3550 inhab. with a sumptuous Baroque church. To the N.E. in the 'Grove of Pomegranates' the quarry is disused that supplied stone for the crypt of Lutyens' Roman Catholic cathedral in Liverpool.

From the w. entrance to the town a by-road runs N. along the ridge, then descends into the Ramla valley. High above the sandy beach of Ramla Bay is *Calypso's Cave*, by tradition the Homeric spot where the Calypso bewitched Odysseus on his way home from the Trojan War.

Other tracks radiate from Nadur through orchards to *San Blas Bay*, and down the Daħlet Qorrot valley, while the road continues to *Qala*, also linked by road with Mġarr.

C To San Lawrenz and Ta' Pinu

The western part of the island, distant from easy landing-places and with its approaches protected by the Kastell, suffered least from piratical incursions and its villages preserve more early buildings. The main road runs N.W., passing the turning for Għasri and Żebbuġ.—At (1½ m.) a fork below the conical truncated hill of Ta Għammar (550 ft) a by-road diverges right to the imposing basilica of **Ta' Pinu**, erected in an eclectic style in 1920–31. It covers the medieval chapel where a local peasant woman heard the voice of the Virgin in 1883. Ex-votos attest various miraculous cures and escapes from misfortune. The church lies between Għammar and Għarb and c. ½ m. from either by track. About 550 yds farther along, the main road again divides. By the right branch we may reach (2½ m.) *Għarb*, while the left branch continues w. to *San Lawrenz*.

A new road descends a steep hill to an area where a number of geological faults combine to make a series of splendid natural features. QALA DWERJA is an almost circular lagoon closed on the seaward side by *Fungus Rock*. The repellent plant which gives the rock its name was successfully dried for use by the Knights as a dressing for wounds and a remedy for dysentery. The plant was gathered by means of a primitive aerial ropeway and the approach guarded by a tower. Near by is *Tieqa Zerqa*, the 'window in the cliff', another natural rock formation. To the N. is *Il-Qawra*, or Kaura, an inland sea to which water (and fishing boats in calm weather) can enter by a fissure in the rock. Its crystal waters make it attractive to swimmers.

Excavations at *Ras Il-Wardija*, on the s.w. promontory of the island, have uncovered a rock-cut Punic temple with an altar on the seaward side.

INDEX

Note: Topographical names are printed in bold type; names of persons in italics; other entries in Roman type.

Printed by Neill & Co. Ltd., Edinburgh